You Don't
Know Jack

Based upon material researched and presented on our YouTube channel, youtube.com/c/chicktracts, from the You Don't Know Jack video series.

For a distributor near you, call (909) 987-0771, or visit www.chick.com

Copyright © 2017 David W. Daniels

Published by:
CHICK PUBLICATIONS
PO Box 3500, Ontario, Calif. 91761-1019 USA
Tel: (909) 987-0771
Fax: (909) 941-8128
Web: www.chick.com
Email: postmaster@chick.com

Printed in the United States of America

ISBN: 978-0-75891-1865

Contents

Introduction

To the world, Jack Chick was an enigma. Some cast him as a purveyor of hate, angrily consigning all rotten sinners to a burning hell.

Others admired his consistency, volumes of gospel tracts with wide ranging stories, invariably ending with a single appeal to be saved.

His courage in exposing false piety and false religions won him notable enemies. But thousands flooded the Chick Publications mail box with gratitude, finally free from their bondage.

To his friends he was generous to a fault. But anyone attempting to divert his life calling met a steely resolve.

Gifted with extraordinary insight and communication skills, his stories rang true to the human heart. And the anointed message pierced deep inside the spirit.

In his death even his enemies begrudgingly acknowledged his impact. Over more than fifty years the tract, *THIS WAS YOUR LIFE* became recognized as the most widely read gospel tract in the history of the world.

Year after year millions of tracts streamed from the Chick printing press. The 50+ year total neared 900 million at the time of Jack's death. Late in Jack's life one reporter surmised that he was probably the most widely read author alive at that time surpassed only by a few dead ones in all of history.

Jack's heart for the lost responded to missionaries appealing for foreign translations by financing the design work for more than a thousand foreign language titles in over a hundred languages.

Files at Chick Publications contain thousands of testimonies sent in over the years. We can only imagine how great the crowd was at His welcome-home party on October 23, 2016, inside the "pearly gates."

In life, some thought they knew Jack. But this book, by someone who knew him well (and researched the rest) goes a long way in setting the record straight. Even others of us who worked almost every day with Jack were surprised by some of the details that David's research revealed.

Please read on to learn more about a man whose sole dedication in life was to persuade you to join him someday in the New Jerusalem.

In loving memory,

George Collins (Jack's Friend)

1

Jaaaaaaack Chiiiiiiiiiiiick!!!!!!

It has been nothing but the greatest pleasure to work with Jack Chick the last 16 years. This is a real man, a regular guy, and a deeply devoted Christian. I have to say "is," because he's, right at this moment, with His Saviour in heaven.

I joked that he might need the Saviour to come over to where he is, because he's probably being mobbed by people who were saved through his Chick tracts!

People like this:

> "Just a testimony to let you know Chick tracts get results. I came across a girl named Carrie. She was very depressed and ready to commit suicide. I had a copy of **Trust Me** which I gave to her and witnessed to her. She accepted the Lord and changed her mind about ending it all. Praise God!"

Or this one:

> "Your pamphlets have been a blessing to many of us. They provide an easy way to get the gospel to a person who can then consider it in privacy or in a spare moment.
>
> I practiced law for 20 years. I kept the tracts on the lobby furniture and several on my desk. One day a young, good-looking flight instructor came in for

6

an appointment: financial problems. Of course I shared with him and he left to go to the airport. On his way out he "stole" a GI Joe tract [***Holy Joe***]. When he got to the airport he had to wait for the mechanic to get the plane gassed up and ready for flight.

He intended to take it up as high as he could over Sky Harbor Airport here in Phoenix and then dive into the runway at a 90 degree angle.

While waiting for the mechanic to finish his tasks, the flight instructor reached in his pocket and took out the GI Joe tract. He read it and with a broken spirit accepted Jesus as his Lord. Sometime later, still under conviction he came in with a nickel and paid for the tract and with it led his buddy (another flight instructor) to the Lord."

These people were spared a Christless, agonizing eternity, because of a given, or well-placed, Chick tract.

I spent the last weeks grieving when we knew we were going to lose Jack. But now that he's in heaven with my praying Grandma, it's hard to be unhappy for him. I'm just being straight with you. He's receiving his rewards in heaven. And to him, the greatest rewards are those people who got saved because Jack cared about them and followed the Lord to reach them.

A few weeks ago, when we were working on a dual-auto-biography together, he called me over and said, "I'm convicted by the scripture, Proverbs 27:2: "Let another man praise thee, and not thine own mouth; a stranger, and not thine own lips."

He said to me, "I can't toot my own horn. So you're gonna

have to toot it for me after I'm gone."

I have told Jack for years how I've watched movies and read articles by all sorts of people saying they knew him. And I told him, someday I'm gonna write a biography of you. And I'm going to say to them, "I know Jack Chick. I've worked with him for years. Jack is my best friend. And *you* don't know Jack."

Would you like to get to know Jack better, like I did?

When Jack first hired me, in August of 2000 (I'll tell you more about that in another chapter —pretty miraculous stuff), the first thing he did was sit me down in his office. And then for the next three days he told me about his life experiences with Christians, Catholics, upbringing, Hollywood,—the works. He told me "the good, the bad, and the ugly," literally. And he also told me some basic things about himself.

For instance, he told me about Paul and Jan Crouch, when they were just starting out TBN, Trinity Broadcasting Network. They were such sweet people, very humble. They'd come out in their little car, I think it was a VW, and pick Jack up and they'd go over to Santa Ana where they were filming their TV show.

Jack used to share his tracts on their show and talk about his desire to win souls for Christ. It was special. But, he said, they were not simple people, at all. They were very shrewd.

Just a few weeks ago we were talking about it again. Jack said he came to TBN to be on a show. He asked them, "Is there a room where I can pray?" He wanted some time with the Lord before he went on the air. So they directed him to a room.

Well, it turns out that the walls were more like paper. He

was praying, when he heard footsteps in the next room. Paul and Jan walked in, talking numbers. He said that Jan was spouting numbers, statistics, figures, so fast, it amazed him. He told me, "She looks folksy. But don't let that fool you. She's a genius with numbers."

Jack learned never to assume anyone is simply like his or her appearance seems to suggest. It was amazing how he would catch what a person was about rather quickly. He had insights that amazed me, and that all went into characters in his tracts.

Jack with Paul and Jan on Praise the Lord, early 1970s

Jack was on Paul and Jan's show a number of times. And they would always ask him about the new tract that he had made... until he published *The Gay Blade.* Then the brakes went on. Paul went to Jack and said, "NO! We can't put that one on the air!"

Jack had no idea why. Paul Crouch explained that there was something called "the fairness doctrine." It demanded that if anyone objected to something being said on a controversial topic, the network had to provide "equal time" to opposing points of view. They didn't want a Christian network to be forced to put homosexual propaganda on its station.

So Jack couldn't show *that* tract on their show. But the others were fine, and people through the 1970s bought all the different tracts and won many to Christ —including me! June 7th, 1972.

But the most amazing TV appearance was one Jack was actually warned about, in advance, by none other than former occultist John Todd. People can say whatever they want to about Todd, but decades later, with all the evidence that has come out, it is hard to prove things he said wrong. And he was proved right on a number of amazing issues he didn't make public. I'll tell you another one later.

Jack was offered to go onto a major Christian TV show on the east coast. John Todd told him, "Jack, don't go. It's a set-up."

This one time Jack didn't listen. The host was a sweet Christian man on TV, always sounding folksy and sincere. But Jack had never met him before. So he went. Jack told me he was assured he'd be met at the airport, taken to his hotel, and well-taken care of.

He wasn't.

Jack got to the airport, and *nobody* met him. He had to find his way through a brand-new city, and eventually found his hotel. Nobody was there to meet him, either.

Then the next morning, while he was having breakfast, a

Catholic priest walked in! He said he was sent by the host and asked Jack all sorts of questions, then he took Jack to the studio.

In the studio, people were talking and joking, a nice banter. Then the host walked in. Suddenly, everyone became silent. Jack wondered why the people would act so intimidated that they couldn't even be themselves around this man.

Jack was told what questions he would be asked. That helped calm him a bit. But he needed to pray. They showed him to the waiting room, called the Green Room. He stayed in the Green Room, praying, until he was called. Then he had to walk through a curtain that was really in front of a wall.

"And here he is, Christian comic artist, Jaaaaaaaack Chiiiiiiiiiiiick!!!!!!"

Jack was so embarrassed. And people didn't really look at him, they looked at the camera, while they talked to him. Very awkward. Like everyone was mugging for camera time.

He told me that when they film you, they have this red light that goes on. That red light tells you which camera is pointed toward you. So this host, though he was supposed to be talking to his guest, would actually turn his head toward the camera with the light!

Jack refused to do it. He made sure that if someone talked to him, Jack turned and looked right back at the person. He was talking to a person, not the audience.

This famous folksy Christian host looked at Jack and said, "Now Jaaaack, why did you draw a comic of a man eating human fingers?"

Jack was flummoxed! That wasn't on the list of questions.

In fact, the host threw away that list and drilled Jack with all sorts of other questions he was not prepared for. That was dirty. He realized at that point that, once again, John Todd was right. He should never have come.

Jack explained how the comic book itself says that the story was based upon an actual event that happened in the latter stages of satanic obsession near Big Sur in 1973. And he did his best to answer the other brand-new questions fired upon him by the host.

Jack felt like a fool. This wasn't Christianity. This was show biz. Jack realized people weren't going to be nice to him if he was going to expose evil and give the gospel.

Jesus said, in John 15:20: "Remember the word that I said unto you, The servant is not greater than his lord. If they have persecuted me, they will also persecute you; if they have kept my saying, they will keep yours also."

Jack didn't do many interviews after that. Instead, he focused on the one thing that made a difference: preaching the gospel. He was a comic artist, so God used him to make comic tracts that preach the gospel.

That is what he lived his life doing until he could not physically do it anymore.

The fact that I was able to write tracts with him the last 16 years was the **second** greatest gift Jack gave me. The first gift Jack gave was writing the tract, ***This Was Your Life***, that motivated a middle-aged man to give it to 9-year-old me, and by which I was saved.

Jack's vision got me saved. I could never repay him for that. But I can continue his vision for the lost.

I pray you also will pick up that vision. Chick tracts **are** controversial, but they are researched (regardless of what the critics say —that's for another chapter), and they are prayed over, from start to finish. We write many different kinds. What works is different for everybody.

I pray you will pick up gospel tracts that do the job for you, that shake up a person to the point that he or she wakes up. We want people to understand that there is a heaven to gain, and a hell to avoid. And there's an eternity coming, either to be grateful and thank God, or to gnaw their tongues in pain for refusing Christ's payment for their sin.

I'll tell you more about Jack in the next chapter.

2

Who's the Real Jesuit?

I didn't learn everything about Jack in the first three days I worked with him, but it sure was a crash-course. You have to realize how incredible it feels to be trusted with so much information. Jack shared his personal life experiences with me. And over time Jack watched me as I researched about what he told me. I'd go and find whatever I could to see if there was evidence from other sources of what Jack told me. In fact, my first job title was Research Consultant.

He used to say, "David, thank God you're not my enemy." Which is ironic, because I used to be his enemy.

I had been a Chick-tract-reading, King-James-Bible-trusting Christian. But by my second semester in Bible college in the Fall of 1981, I had become a New American Standard reader, who quickly became suspicious of all things Chick.

You know how that happened?

I trusted men.

Psalm 118:8-9 says "It is better to trust in the LORD than to put confidence in man. It is better to trust in the LORD than to put confidence in princes."

And do you know the thing that turned me into an anti-Chick zealot? It was an article in *Christianity Today* by Gary

Metz against a man named Alberto Rivera, who claimed to be a former Jesuit priest.

Gary Metz around 2007, AKA "Doctorzin" on YouTube

Christianity Today, **March 13, 1981, with the Gary Metz article against Alberto Rivera**

I photocopied the *Christianity Today* version of the article and carried it around with me for years in my backpack, showing it to people, telling them how bad Chick was. From a guy saved by a Chick tract and who returned to the Lord with Chick tracts, I had become an enemy of Jack Chick.

Jack was vilified in the press. He was made out to be a fire-breathing villain, as if he hated everyone and everything that wasn't exactly like him.

But that wasn't Jack at all. In the 16 years I've worked here I've learned what kind of Christian Jack was and how consistent Jack stayed. That consistent Christianity was witnessed for over 48 years, according to his own friends, friends that I know. The *real* Jack Chick was part of what turned me back into a soul winner who uses Chick tracts every day to reach others for Christ.

Want to learn more about the *real* Jack Chick? Those of you who know me or have watched my vlogs, know that I care a lot about *fruit*. Jesus said, in Matthew 7:16-20:

Ye shall know them by their fruits. Do men gather
grapes of thorns, or figs of thistles? Even so every
good tree bringeth forth good fruit; but a corrupt
tree bringeth forth evil fruit. A good tree cannot
bring forth evil fruit, neither *can* a corrupt tree
bring forth good fruit. Every tree that bringeth not
forth good fruit is hewn down, and cast into the
fire. Wherefore by their fruits ye shall know them.

So when I believed the anti-Chick, anti-Alberto articles,
I became Jack's enemy. First, I photocopied that *Christianity Today* article. Then I started showing that article to
anyone and everyone. Never mind that the article had no
actual documentation, nor has it ever shown a single proven
charge against Alberto, from 1981 to 2016. Never mind that
Metz claimed he had proof and promised to produce it, but
never did.

Christianity Today was a trusted magazine. So I trusted
the article and a guy no one had ever heard of before. And
as a result, I stopped handing out Chick tracts. Completely.
Plus, my professors criticized the gospel message on the
back page.

Oh, and I believed my professors, too. In fact, I stopped
handing out *any* tracts at all. Where I could have passed out
thousands upon thousands of Chick gospel tracts to unsaved
people, from 1981 through 1998, 17 years, I stopped passing
tracts.

Because of a hit piece in a big Christian magazine, I stopped
passing tracts. And Brothers and Sisters, that is the goal of the
Ecumenical Movement. "Don't you dare try to evangelize our
brother and sister Catholics. We're all one big, happy family!"
That's the Ecumenical Movement in a nutshell.

Now, one day I was in the office here at Chick Publications, researching something on a totally different topic for Jack. Then I found an article where someone denied that some Jesuit was connected to CRI, the Christian Research Institute, started by the late Dr. Walter Martin.

That got my attention. You see, one of the things Jack had told me, was that Alberto had said something about a Jesuit he recognized connected with CRI, so I was intrigued. The man was a Jesuit priest named Mitchell Pacwa, SJ. So I searched online and found a book published by CRI called *The Cult of the Virgin: Catholic Mariology and the Apparitions of Mary*, by Elliot Miller and Kenneth R. Samples. It came out in 1992.

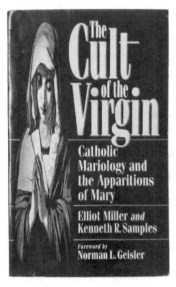

The CRI book on Mary, featuring Norman Geisler and Jesuit Mitchel Pacwa

It has a Foreword written by Norman Geisler, who got his Ph.D. from the Jesuit Loyola University of Chicago. But look at the end of the book. Appendix B is a Response to the book by Jesuit Mitchell Pacwa.

It turns out that he was a professor of Theology at—Loyola University of Chicago, the same place where Norman Geisler got his Ph.D back in the late 1960s!

Let me read to you what the authors wrote about Jesuit

priest Mitchell Pacwa and the purpose of their 1992 book on Mary. This is from page 161.

> As was stated in the introduction, the underlying purpose of this book is ultimately ecumenical rather than anti-ecumenical: to promote open dialogue and understanding among Catholics and Protestants about an issue that continues to separate them.
>
> To better serve this purpose we asked Father Mitchell Pacwa, S.J., a Scripture scholar from Loyola University at Chicago, if we might include his thoughts and criticisms regarding our book within its pages. He graciously agreed to do so.

Wow. So already they are ecumenical. They want Catholic and Protestants together. So I guess they didn't try to get this Jesuit priest saved. Let me go on.

> Pacwa is an able scholar and apologist whose manner of life evidences (get this) a strong personal relationship with Christ.

Really? Which Christ? Christ of the Bible, or the Christ of Catholicism? They're not the same.

> We have enjoyed with him the kind of relationship we advocate between Bible-believing Catholics and Protestants: honest and respectful discussion of our differences, but also positive fellowship in Christ and cooperative efforts in the common cause of Christ's kingdom.

So Jesuit, call-no-man-father Mitchell Pacwa, is a "Bible-believing Catholic," with a "strong personal relationship with Christ"? And Pacwa is a "scripture scholar"?

Could I have been wrong? Is the Ecumenical Movement

actually good? Was Alberto in error? Was he just a rabble rouser? Or, was Alberto actually right? I had to find out more about Jesuit priest Mitchell Pacwa.

I found a book Pacwa wrote, just four years after the CRI book, entitled, "Father, Forgive Me, for I Am Frustrated: Growing in Faith When You Don't Find It Easy Being Catholic."[1]

Look at page 34:

> For example, the consequence of sin is a central theme of St. Ignatius of Loyola's *Spiritual Exercises*, a classic manual for directing retreats, which has been a powerful means of conversion for four hundred years.

So Jesuit priest Mitchell Pacwa isn't interested in dialogue. He's interested in making people Roman Catholic. And how have the Jesuits been making people Catholic for over 400 years? "Ignatius of Loyola's *Spiritual Exercises.*"

So maybe the Ecumenical Movement is really about getting Christians to drop their guard so the Catholics can "dialogue" —that's a Jesuit code word for getting others to compromise with Rome. And does it stop there? No. They use spiritual retreats to actually try to turn Christians into Catholics!

One of my first classes at Fuller Seminary in the fall of 1984 was called Spiritual Formation and Discipleship. It was led by a famous Presbyterian minister. And one of the things he told us was that the Jesuits had made a special ar-

---

1) *Father, Forgive Me, for I Am Frustrated: Growing in Faith When You Don't Find It Easy Being Catholic*, by Mitch Pacwa, S.J. (Ann Arbor, Michigan: Charis Books, "an imprint of Servant Publications especially designed to serve Roman Catholics," 1st Printing 1996).

rangement for Fuller seminary students to go, for I think it
was up to a month, to a Jesuit retreat and learn contempla-
tive Christianity with the monks as guides, using something
called the *Spiritual Exercises*.

Do any Fuller grads out there remember that class? Fall
of 1984.

But if the Jesuits were guides, we aren't giving them the
gospel of Jesus Christ that frees them from Mary, the pope,
the saints, the angels, the idolatry and their bondage to
Rome. No, instead, the Jesuits are using the *Spiritual Exercises* to make Catholics out of Christians!

And way back in 1980 Jack Chick took a stand against the
Ecumenical Movement, and never ever changed his stance.
Do you see why? The Roman Catholics are trying to create
a one-world religion —a one-world Catholic religion. Jack
wasn't against the Ecumenical Movement because he hated
people. Jack was against the Ecumenical Movement because
he was desperate for souls to be saved.

But the Ecumenical Movement STOPS evangelism of
the precious Roman Catholics, and others, as they expand
their movement.

And don't be fooled. The Ecumenical Movement does
not stop by telling Christians not to evangelize Catholics.
It's actually about Catholics trying to turn Christians into
Catholics, or to allow others to become Catholics without
warning them of the eternal consequences.

Look in the news right now. I can guarantee you that the
pope and Protestants and even Baptists are talking about
"ecumenical fellowship."

How about this, from the *Catholic Herald*, November 1st,

2016? Pope Francis just offered to add 6 new Beatitudes to Jesus' list in the Sermon on the Mount. Here are numbers 3 and 6.

3) "Blessed are those who see God in every person and strive to make others also discover him."

Nope. God is not in every person. Romans 8:9 says "... Now if any man have not the Spirit of Christ, he is none of his." Only saved people get to have the Spirit of Christ.

And Pope Francis' Beatitude number 6, "Blessed are those who pray and work for full communion between Christians." That really means Catholics, Orthodox, Protestants, Baptists, and maybe even Mormons, all under one roof.

But Jack, for 56 years, kept his eyes on one goal: winning as many people as possible to salvation by faith in the shed blood of the Lord Jesus, the Son of God, *with nothing added* and nothing taken away.

Proverbs 11:30 is absolutely true: "The fruit of the righteous *is* a tree of life; and he that winneth souls *is* wise." Chick Publications has its eyes on that one goal. The *fruit* of winning souls. Every other thing we do helps us get to that goal.

Working with Jack was like getting on a soul-winning train. I could get on with him and start winning souls, or he would go on without me. Thank God I got on the train with him. I hope I can make up for the years of not passing out tracts.

Maybe as you become more confident, you will too.

To get to know Jack, you don't just get to know a soul winner. You get the opportunity to become a soul winner.

And Chick Publications is here to help you do just that.

3

Two Secrets Shared with Jack

When researching what people *truly* believe, one of the better places to find it is wherever they wrote or spoke to people who were on their side. That is when they are the most comfortable. And that is when they let the most important and personal information slip out.

Another place to find true beliefs is when people confide a fact to you, but they have absolutely nothing to gain by saying it. It doesn't give them money, power, influence or anything else. They didn't make it public. But it didn't make you trust them more or give them anything, either. So they had nothing to gain by saying it. Still, it was something they *had* to tell someone, even if nobody else would listen.

Jack told me a number of them. I will share two of them with you right now. Would you like to hear two secrets?

Let me start with John Todd.

Those who have seen my vlogs or read my books know that I don't take research lightly. My family will tell you, I live research. I test assumptions and check for data constantly.

I never met John Todd. I only heard what he has said in public. And all I can say is, I haven't yet found evidence that what he said was wrong. In fact, he seems to have known data that didn't even become moderately public for decades after he said them.

Jack shot this pose of John Todd for page 11 of the Crusader Comic *Spellbound*

Some of you have asked me, do you think he did the bad things they said he did? I would answer this way: Let's say someone knew the things it seems he did. And he was unafraid to tell those things. Do you think the powers that be would leave him free to keep doing it? Or do you think they would figure a way to silence him or at least put him away and prevent him from talking?

Something to think about.

One day John Todd took Jack aside in private, and told him this: "The biggest battle of the end of the 20th century will be the battle for the King James Bible."

John didn't say, "Illuminati." He didn't say "witchcraft." He didn't even say "politics" or "one world government" or "one world religion." He said, "The biggest battle of the end of the 20th century will be the battle for the King James Bible."

And he was right.

The second person was Alberto Rivera Romero, former Jesuit priest. He told Jack a secret regarding the many Bible versions starting to flood the market to replace the King James.

When Jack began to work with Alberto, it created a fire

storm. Alberto had tried several ways to get his story out, but had been shouted down by the Catholic-infected Christian media and no one would touch him who depended on their denomination for support.

Since he was an independent publisher, Chick didn't answer to any of them. Jack prayed and God said do it.

Jack obeyed, as was his pattern in life.

But guess what? It turns out that there was solid evidence for Alberto's claims. Over the years, other documents have surfaced. When I began this book I did some more digging and continued to uncover more. Here are some that you can see for yourself:

Ex-Jesuit Alberto Rivera Romero

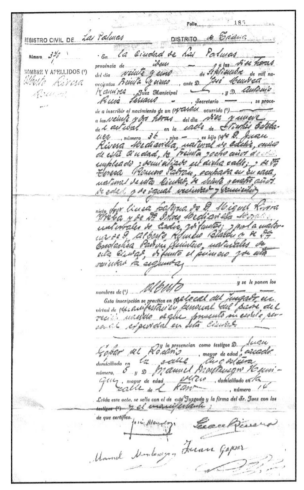

Alberto Rivera's Birth Certificate, September 19, 1935

Unlike some people around today, I actually have his birth certificate.

Alberto's letter from the Ministry of Justice of Madrid, February 26, 1955

I also have the letter from the Ministry of Justice of Madrid, certifying Alberto for a visa.

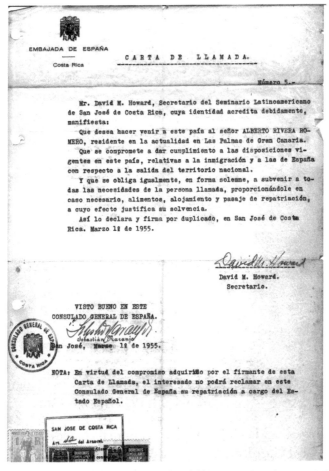

Seminary request for a visa for Alberto, March 10, 1955

I have the request from the Latin American Seminary in San José, Costa Rica, requesting a visa for Alberto.

Alberto's Good Conduct Letter from the Civil Guard, March 14, 1955

I have the March 14th 1955 letter from the 212th Brigade of the Civil Guard, declaring that Alberto had "good, and moral conduct, both privately and publicly, and lacks any previous record for being involved in any social or political situation." That exempted him from any military service, and gave him permission to move from the Canary Islands to Costa Rica.

I even have documentation of one mistake Alberto made.

Gary Metz's articles against Alberto claimed there was a "missing year," after Alberto spoke in Guatemala and revealed who he was, as cited on page 29 (30 in new printings) of the Chick Crusaders Comic, *Alberto*.

That's because it wasn't 1965 when he spoke to them. It was November 20-27, 1966. He had the proof for years with him, but never bothered to check it himself. When he'd finish talking to Jack, he'd wave his hand and say, "It is done," and walk out of the room.

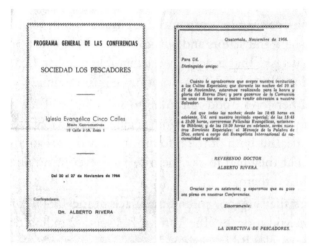

Guatemala Conference Program Listing Rivera, November 20-27, 1966

But here is the program for the conference, listing Alberto as one of the speakers. "Sociedad los Pescadores," Iglesia Evangélica Cinco Calles, in Guatemala City, November 20-27, 1966, "Conferenciante Dr. Alberto Rivera." So I fixed Alberto's error in later printings of the comic. Now it says "Guatemala, Nov. 1966."

So I know a lot more about Alberto.

And once again, I have to tell you, I never met Alberto. But I know people who knew Alberto. And one of the things that Alberto Rivera said, I disagreed with. I've disagreed with a few of his opinions. I've disagreed with a few things he was told or taught. But I haven't yet found him to be in an error of fact.

Jack told me that Alberto said privately: "The Vatican has spent 2 billion dollars to create false Bible versions." Run the numbers, from the 1800s to the present. Think of all the jobs, companies, corporations, buy-outs, colleges, books, publishers, translators and outright Catholic agents working on that task. That is actually a believable number. (Look at the vlog, "It's a Job," if you want more information.) [2]

Neither John Todd nor Alberto sold Bibles. They didn't get any Brownie points for going against the flow of modern versions. But both of them found these two facts so important that they had to say them to Jack, even if no one else ever heard them.

Here they are, one more time. Back in the 1980s Alberto Rivera said to Jack, "The Vatican has spent 2 billion dollars to create false Bible versions."

And in the 1970s, John Todd said to Jack: "The biggest battle of the end of the 20th century will be the battle for the King James Bible."

Jack knew these things for years. It fueled his insistence on using the King James in our tracts. And it helped him to encourage me to continue studying the King James issue. You are still seeing the results of continuing research today.

Slice it however you want. The fact is, Jack had it right all along.

---

2) Found at https://youtu.be/oFnzx_yiFbI

4

A Man of Prayer

Jack Chick was a man of prayer. For 16 years, Jack and I would start the day by getting before the Lord in prayer. We'd start our work by praying to the Lord. And whenever we got bogged down, it was back to our knees. Chick Publications has been run by prayer for 56 years.

And while so many other companies have compromised or become cultic or outright disappeared, Chick Publications is still here, hasn't changed, and it's still run by prayer. Someone was doing something right.

When Gary Metz wrote the articles in *Cornerstone* magazine about former Jesuit, Alberto Rivera, he made fun of Jack saying that he prayed about Alberto and that the Lord told him to work with him.

Cornerstone no longer exists, but you can find it on the Wayback machine.[3] (I have to tell you, I'm amazed at Metz's lack of documentation.)

Metz wrote: "What does Jack Chick think about this? … When he was finally reached by phone at his home, he said … that he knows Alberto's story is true because he 'prayed about it.'"

I have a sneaking suspicion that's not what Jack actually said.

---

3) See https://web.archive.org/web/20051202084221/http://www.cornerstonemag.com/pages/show_page.asp?228

But since that is the story, we'll go with those words. Anyone who knows Jack, knows he most definitely prayed about it.

In the light of the hearsay presented in the articles against Jack, Alberto and others, who could blame the doubters? Alberto said some pretty wild things in his stories. And as far back as the early 1980s, I went against Jack and Chick tracts as a result of those stories, and especially the hit pieces against Jack.

But what if we could verify, in an official document that I found, whether Alberto told the truth about one crucial story? It just so happens that I have that document. And I will show it to you.

From the time I came to work with Jack in August of 2000, people who have known Jack for decades said the same thing. Jack is a man of prayer. He would come to them and say the Lord showed something to him in prayer. And they'd wonder, "Where did that come from?"

Over time, they watched as the things Jack said —happened, or were proven true. And over the years, people began to have their own doubts replaced with, "I guess Jack really does hear from God."

Others simply made fun of him.

So let me ask you: Was Jack's trust in his prayers misplaced? It's 2016. Can we verify any of it?

Here's just one example. In the *Alberto* comic, Alberto claims to have wreaked havoc at the Bible college he attended. On page 24, Alberto says this: "When the school officials tried to get me sent out of the country, the Vatican, through the government of Spain, claimed I was an army deserter. I was removed before they could discover I was a Jesuit."

I showed you in the last chapter, that Alberto attended

the Seminario Bíblico Latinoamericano in San José, Costa Rica. I showed you the official government documents from Spain, the Spanish Embassy, and the Canary Islands, that said Alberto had *no* public or private record against him.

One was from the Ministry of Justice in Madrid, February 26, 1955: Alberto was neither a convicted offender nor a fugitive. He had no criminal record. One was from the Embassy of Spain in Costa Rica on March 1st, 1955, where David Howard, the Secretary of the Seminario Latinoamericano promised to take care of Alberto.

And one even came from Don Jose Gonzalez Herrera, the Commander of the Civil Guard at the Garrison in Puerto de la Luz, Las Palmas, Canary Islands, Alberto's home town. It said he had no public or private dings on his record. If he were a draft-dodger or a deserter, *this guy would know it*. It's dated March 14, 1955.

Now Alberto's visa to leave Las Palmas was authorized for only *3 months*, beginning February 26, 1955. That means that Alberto had to leave for Costa Rica by or before May 26, 1955. All these documents are dated from late February to Mid-March 1955.

So by May 1955, Alberto was in San José, Costa Rica, as a Bible college student. He had no criminal or any other kind of record against him. But even according to his old friend, Plutarco Bonilla, who later became a leader in the United Bible Societies, he made trouble while he was there, just like Alberto said.

If he got kicked out, then the head of the Bible college would rescind his support, and say "I'm not gonna support Alberto anymore," and he'd be sent back home to the Canary Islands. Let's just say that the Vatican *did* want Alberto to quickly get away from the Bible college, no questions asked. How would they do it?

This document may have the answer.

It's dated September 29, 1956, only about a year and a half after Alberto got his visa. It's written in high-sounding speech. But here is the document.

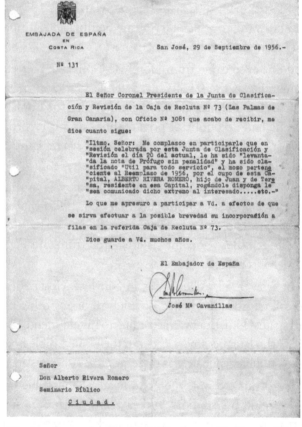

EMBAJADA DE ESPAÑA
EN
COSTA RICA

San José, 29 de Septiembre de 1956.-

Nº 131

El Señor Coronel Presidente de la Junta de Clasificación y Revisión de la Caja de Recluta Nº 73 (Las Palmas de
Gran Canaria), con Oficio Nº 3081 que acabo de recibir, me
dice cuanto sigue:

"Iltmo. Señor: Me complazco en participarle que en
"sesión celebrada por esta Junta de Clasificación y
"Revisión el día 20 del actual, le ha sido "levanta-
"da la nota de Prófugo sin penalidad" y ha sido cla-
"sificado "Util para todo servicio", el mozo pertene
"ciente al Reemplazo de 1956, por el cupo de esta Ca-
"pital, ALBERTO RIVERA ROMERO, hijo de Juan y de Tere
"sa, residente en esa Capital, rogándole disponga le
"sea comunicado dicho extremo al interesado.....eto.-"

Lo que me apresuro a participar a Vd. a efectos de que
se sirva efectuar a la posible brevedad su incorporación a
filas en la referida Caja de Recluta Nº 73.

Dios guarde a Vd. muchos años.

El Embajador de España

José Mª Cavanillas

Señor
Don Alberto Rivera Romero
Seminario Bíblico
Ciudad.

**Notice from the Spanish Embassy in Costa Rica
that Alberto is no longer a "deserter"**

Here is a literal translation.

Embajada de España en Costa Rica No. 131	Embassy of Spain in Costa Rica No. 131
San José, 29 de Septiembre de 1956.	San Jose, 29th of September, 1956
El Señor Coronel Presidente de la Junta de Clasificación y Revisión de la Caja de Recluta Número 73 (Las Palmas de Gran Canaria), con Oficio Número 3081 que acabo de recibir, me dice cuanto sigue:	The Honorable Colonel Chairman of the Board of Classification and Review of Induction Station Number 73 (Las Palmas of the Grand Canary [Islands]), with Office 3081 that number just received, tells me the following:
"Iltmo. Senor: Me complazco en participarle que en sesión celebrada por esta Junta de Clasificación y Revisión el día 20 del actual, le ha sido "levantada la nota de Prófugo sin penalidad" y ha sido clasificado "Util para todo servicio", el marzo perteneciente al Reemplazo de 1956, por el cupo de esta Capital, ALBERTO RIVERA ROMERO, hijo de Juan y de Teresa, residente en esa Capital, rogándole disponga le sea comunicado dicho extremo al interesado.....etc."	"Most Illustrious Sir: I am pleased to participate in a meeting held by this Board of Classification and Review on the 20th of the current [month], "the notice of Deserter has been lifted without penalty" and he [Alberto] has been classified "Useful for all service" regarding the March Replacement of 1956, for the quota of this Capital, Alberto Rivera Romero, son of Juan and Teresa, who lives in this Capital, requesting this saying be communicated to the interested party.....etc."
Lo que me apresuro a participar a Vd. a efectos de que se sirva efectuar a la posible brevedad su incorporación a filas en la referida Caja de Recluta Número 73.	That which I hasten you to participate in order that it may be useful to carry out for your earliest possible induction in the [previously] referenced Induction Station Number 73.
Dios guarde a Vd. muchos años.	God keep you many years [to come].
El Embajador de España José Ma Cavanillas	The Ambassador of Spain, [Signed] José Maria Cavanillas

Sr.
Don Alberto Rivera Romero
Seminario Bíblico
    Ciudad
	Mr.
	Don Alberto Rivera Romero
	Seminario Bíblico
	    City

Literal translation of the Spanish letter.

And here is a summary.

The Colonel Chairman of the Board of Classification and Review of Induction Station Number 73, from Las Palmas Canary Islands, sent a special letter to the Spanish Ambassador of Costa Rica, who forwarded the message to Alberto at the Bible college.

It said this: You are no longer labeled a "Deserter" or "Fugitive," *Prófugo*. Now you are labeled "Useful for all service," *Util para todo servicio*. You can still be a part of the March 1956 recruitment, if you rush home, basically.

So, since it's already 6 months later, September, the Ambassador says literally, "I hasten you to participate in order that it may be useful to carry out for your earliest possible induction in the [previously] referenced Induction Station (*Caja de Recluta*) Number 73." Signed, José Maria Cavanillas, Ambassador of Spain.

In other words, Don't delay, Alberto, you're already six months late for your draft. Get out of Costa Rica and go home to the Canary Islands, *now*!

I have gone over and over this document. It's just as official as the earlier one from the Secretary of the Bible seminary. The only problem is, Alberto **wasn't** a draft-dodger. He wasn't a **deserter**. But this letter **did** get Alberto **out** of that Bible seminary lickety-split!

This letter was genuine. But it was clearly a **ruse**. Someone at the Spanish Embassy, or back home in Las Palmas, or somewhere, wanted Alberto **out** of that Bible seminary. Was it before they could discover Alberto was really a Jesuit on a Jesuitical mission?

The power of the Spanish military backed Alberto's recall notice. This says he was **drafted**! But guess what? There is **no** documentation that Alberto went back to the Canary Islands at this point. Alberto should have raced back home. But he didn't. Do you get why? ***Alberto knew the letter was a ruse, to get him out of the Seminario Bíblico Latinoamericano.***

And guess what? I have documentation of where Alberto

did go. And it *wasn't* back home. In fact, Alberto didn't even leave Costa Rica! But I'll tell about that in another chapter.

The bottom line is this: I have been able to document not only Alberto's statements about Rome and the Jesuits, but also his own testimony. To this date his testimony has stood up to documented facts.

I think Jack **did** hear from God. I think God **did** delay the Whore of Babylon's agenda because Jack published Alberto's testimony.

But there is a lot more to Jack than just exposing Rome. I'll tell more about that side of Jack in the next chapter.

5

Jack: A Generous Man of His Word

Jack with wife Lola Lynn - 1980s

Jack was a very kind and generous man. And Jack kept his word, no matter what.

I don't say those words lightly. Over 45 years ago Jack said to a man I knew, "Work with me, and you'll never go hungry." And he kept his word through the decades that followed through thick and thin, even to that man's old age. Jack put his money —and his actions— where his mouth was.

Jack was an example of what a godly man should be, as it says in Psalm 15:4 "…He that sweareth to *his own* hurt, and changeth not."

Jack showed kindness to others, regardless of whether his kindness was repaid or not. Most everyone at Chick Publications could tell you their own personal stories. But let me give you just a couple of examples, both my own, and that of a former Catholic priest.

Skinny me - November 3rd, 2003

It is so wonderful to finally be able to do this! Even when it was difficult, Jack didn't back out when he gave his word.

When Jack and I started working together in August of 2000, my metabolism was very high. I walked fast, talked fast, and I burned calories like I was a fireplace. In the dead of winter, I warmed the people who were next to me. I didn't even need a jacket. Jack knew something was wrong.

Here's a picture of me from 2003, shortly after we finished Jack's film, *The Light of the World*. When I showed this picture to Jack, he said, "You look like Death." All I needed was a hood and a scythe, especially when you see the picture in black and white.

"BUT GOD SAID UNTO HIM, THOU FOOL, THIS NIGHT THY SOUL SHALL BE REQUIRED OF THEE:"
Luke 12:20

Death portrayed by Jack in *This Was Your Life*

I should have listened to Jack and gone to the doctor. But I held off going for another year, until late 2004. By then the doctor told me I was hyperthyroid, and off the charts. On a scale from 1-12, I was a 20. I started losing as much as a pound a day. My doctor said I had "muscular myopathy." My body was burning even my muscles.

I was 42 and my doctor said my body was killing me. I trembled when I walked. So 80 year old Jack held *me* up! I got to repay him 10 years later, when he was 90, and I got to help hold him up. It was the least I could do.

Jack lent countless people money. He hated money, except for what it could do to help people. One day in the 1980s Alberto Rivera brought a man to meet Jack. He said his name was Lee Abeyta. He was a former Catholic priest and homosexual. As a result, he had, as Romans 1 says, "dishonoured his body" and was reaping what he had sown.

He had some serious personal medical issues. But as a former priest (vow of poverty and all), he had no money to take care of himself. Jack talked privately with Alberto.

"What if he's a Catholic plant?" There was, of course, the real possibility that he was sent there to cause problems at Chick Publications. Alberto replied, "What if he's for real? You've got to take the chance."

Back then not many were going to help a former priest in trouble. After the 2nd Vatican Council ended in 1965, most churches started "making nice" with Catholicism. Christian bookstore magazines advised Bible bookstores to start stocking Catholic items, like idols of Mary, Joseph, female-looking angels, sometimes even rosaries.

And, of course, they **had** to stock the official Roman Catholic New American Bible, which included folktales of the Apocrypha. Christians were compromising with Catholicism like never before.

So who else would work with this messed-up man? Jack decided to help him. He took what money he had and paid for the former priest's medical bills, even though they were the result of his "lifestyle." Lee might have even worked at Chick Publications a short while.

And of course, Jack prayed for and about this former priest. One day Jack walked up to Lee and said to him, "The Lord told me you will betray me."

The man's eyes grew wide like saucers. He had the "How did you know?" look. Not long after that Lee disappeared. Then a phone call came. "Who's gonna pay for the repair bill on this car?" It was a radiator shop —in Alaska. Lee had "borrowed" an old car from Jack, and taken off for Alaska with "a male friend." Then the radiator blew.

Those were the Alaskan pipeline days, and everything was way overpriced. The bill came to over $400. So Lee's "partner" handed a credit card. The repairman called to check with the credit card company for a large bill like that. Guess what? The credit card was *stolen* —just like the car!

So the repairman called the cops and they arrested the former priest and his friend. And he put the car up on blocks. That old car wasn't worth retrieving. So here at Chick Publications they said, "We'll sell you the car for the cost of the repair bill." So they sent the guy the pink slip, and he called it even.

You know, sometimes there really is such a thing as poetic justice. Can you imagine the day those two got out of jail? Boy, were they in for a surprise. They were in Alaska, and now they had no car! It had been sold out from under them! They had to laugh about it here at Chick Publications.

So Jack has been betrayed before. But that didn't stop him from trying to help wherever he could.

James 2:15-17 says: "If a brother or sister be naked, and destitute of daily food, And one of you say unto them, Depart in peace, be *ye* warmed and filled; notwithstanding ye give them not those things which are needful to the body; what doth it profit? Even so faith, if it hath not works, is dead, being alone."

Jack had a living faith, and was not afraid to help people, even when the Lord told him that person would betray him.

No story about Jack would be close to accurate, unless it included Jack's generosity.

6

Hitting the Whore of Babylon

Jack at the Royal Tahitian in Ontario, California

As I told you in the last chapter, Jack was very generous. A lot of people in the area in the 1970s already knew of Jack's generosity and kindness.

In fact, Jack told me that a lot of the area pastors would show up to visit Jack – just before lunchtime. And they were more than happy to partake of Jack's giving nature by letting him pay for the bill, for all of them, all of the time.

And Jack never complained. He was kind and paid the bill. Maybe they thought he was rich. (I'll tell you more about that false assumption another time.)

Back to the story. This continued a number of years, until Jack decided to expose the Roman Catholic system. Then, Jack didn't see hide nor hair of those... friends.

Two years after Alberto first came out, one of them called him on the phone. "Jack. Are you still around?"

Jack said, "I'm still around. Where have you been?"

Jack kept to his task, writing gospel tracts and telling Alberto's story, even when his own friends deserted him. Some folks doubted when Jack said the Lord told him to work with Alberto and publish his story.

So, I've been trying to put together what I can of Alberto's story. And I've been thinking about a note Alberto wrote to his father, on the back of an interesting photograph. This might unlock what happened to Alberto after he left the Seminario Biblico Latinoamericano.

Would you like to see what I found?

Alberto Rivera had told Jack, "If you expose the Whore of Babylon, it may cost you your company, your wife, your daughter, your friends, —everything."

Jack really thought about whether he was going to do this or not. He went to his friend, Jim Franklin, who worked here at Chick.

Jack said, "What do you think? Should I hit the Whore?"

Jim said, "Jack, greater is He that is in you, than in the

whole Roman Catholic institution!" Jim quoted scripture whenever he could, which was most of the time.

Well, Jack went into prayer and asked the Lord. And the Lord told him, "Yes."

Jack's old friend, Jim Franklin

From the very beginning, Jack would mail out a letter with his newest gospel tract. So he wrote a letter and mailed it out, saying that he was declaring war on the Whore of Babylon.

One of the largest Catholic newspapers, *Our Sunday Visitor*, then wrote in their next issue that Jack Chick was declaring war on Roman Catholicism. But Jack didn't say, "Roman Catholicism." He said, "The Whore of Babylon."

They knew who they were.

So Jack published Alberto's story. And the rest is history.

What should I do? The scripture is clear:

Proverbs 18:13 "He that answereth a matter before he heareth it, it is folly and shame unto him."

I don't want to sit here with all these documents and not even let the papers and pictures tell their own story. And I certainly don't want to be foolish or shameful. So here I am today, trying to piece together what I can, from what I can find of Alberto.

Among the documents that Alberto left behind, I found a photo of Alberto and some other people. I wondered, can I find any of these people today? I was especially intrigued by what was written on the back of that photograph.

Here it is, possibly for the first time in public:

Alberto in an old photograph

Look at that picture. There are a number of students of different backgrounds, all at a library, working on a table. On the right side, there are two young men. One has a pen and is drawing out something on a huge map, while the second man looks on. Two women and a young man are writing, and a second young man is typing.

Now look at the two guys on the left. The one on the end with a mustache has scooted his chair next to the other one. He's comfortable and smiling and looking at something he's holding.

The other young man with the black jacket and glasses is also smiling. His right hand is right next to the end guy. They are looking at something together. His head is tilted to his left. He is relaxed. Now look at his feet. They are crossed. He isn't going anywhere. He is very comfortable.

So what is happening in this picture? There are either a number of different projects, or different aspects of one project, being worked on. Everyone's papers are on top of the others, which indicates that they are using what they can of all the documents. These clearly look like students doing a joint project. It reminds me of seminary days at Fuller.

Now look above the two on the left. There is a pen-written star on top of each of their heads. Can you figure out who they are?

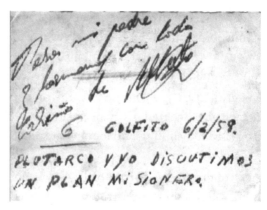

The back of Alberto's photograph

Now look at the back of the photo. The handwriting isn't super-clear, but it's to "mi padre," his father, and someone else, "con todo caliento de Alberto," "with warm affection from Alberto." Underneath is the location: Golfito. That's in Costa Rica, about 188 miles south of the Seminario Latino-americano in San José. So now Alberto is in Golfito.

Map from San José to Golfito, Costa Rica

But look at the date: 6/2/58. The 6th of February, 1958 is a year and a half after Alberto hastily left the Seminario.

And look at what Alberto wrote below: "Plutarco y yo discutimos un plan misionero," (Plutarco and I are discussing a missionary plan.) That is certainly what it looks like. Especially when you know this is a Methodist school of some kind.

But let me back up. I sent this photo to a missionary friend of mine. He wrote back to me, "If this is who I think it is, it's Mr. Plutarco Bonilla, of the United Bible Societies of Costa Rica."

So now I had two questions. Could this be Plutarco Bonilla? And if so, what can I find out from him?

I'd love to take you on the whole journey to finding information, but let me sum up. I looked up everything I could about this Plutarco Bonilla Acosta. And here is what he said in various interviews, translated into English, over the years.

He was born December 2nd 1935. Alberto was born September 19th, 2½ months before Plutarco. And guess what? They were both from Las Palmas of the Grand Canary Islands! Plutarco was baptized in what seems to have been the only Evangelical church in the town when he was 15, about 1951.

Alberto and Plutarco boarding a ship from Las Palmas to Venezuela, May 1955

Here is a photo of Alberto and Plutarco from 1955. They took a ship to Venezuela, then to Costa Rica, arriving in

May 1955, just like I had guessed.

In 1957 Plutarco married Marta Fernandez of Chile and had 3 children. She sadly died in 1963. He later married Esperanza Rios of Costa Rica.

Plutarco was a constant traveler. He studied at Princeton, Athens, Greece, Madrid, and taught in three different American colleges and seminaries. He went on to be pastor of the Methodist church in San José and an advisor for the 1995 revision of the Reina Valera for the United Bible Societies.

Plutarco earned a Master's of Theology at Princeton and a degree in Philology, Linguistics and Literature from the University of Costa Rica. In 2014 he was awarded an honorary Doctorate of Divinity by the South Florida Center for Theological Studies.

And after all his travels and work, Plutarco came back to Costa Rica and became the Rector of the Seminario Bíblico Latinoamericano.

So was it actually THIS Plutarco that is in Alberto's photo that he sent to his dad? It sure looks like the earlier photo of Alberto and Plutarco.

So I put the word out, and a brother sent me Plutarco's email address. I asked him some questions. He was extremely kind and wrote me right back! He wrote, "Long time ago, and for very serious reasons, I decided not to speak to any person about Mr. Rivera."

But he did tell me two things in his letters, just a couple of days ago: 1) He and Alberto did come together to the SBL (Seminario Bíblico Latinoamericano). So that photo by the boat is a genuine one of Alberto and Plutarco.

2. Plutarco wrote, "I cannot remember the exact dates of

my visiting Golfito, but certainly I didn't go there to study, just to preach in the Methodist Church during Holy Week. (In Costa Rica I have studied in the SBL and in the UCR [University of Costa Rica] only)."

So now we know Plutarco **did** visit the Methodist group in Golfito, where Alberto was. We know Alberto is on the end. So that is **indeed** Plutarco right next to him.

There are only two problems.

1) February 6th isn't "holy week." That was Palm Sunday to Easter, March 30th to April 6th, 1958.

So either a) Alberto was off on the picture by two months, which would mean Alberto's school was in session during Holy Week, which isn't likely, or b) Plutarco came down a previous time and visited Alberto on the 6th of February, 1958.

2) If Plutarco wasn't a student, what was he doing discussing a missionary plan with Alberto? Was he just a visitor? He's just younger than Alberto, so he's not his supervisor.

Now take a look at one more thing.

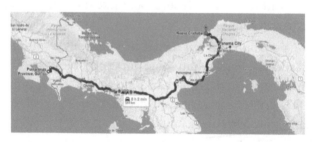

Map from Golfito to Nuevo Cristóbal, Colon, Panama

In 1958, that same year, was the 35th Annual Session of the Provisional Annual Conference of Central America, of the Methodist Episcopal Church, which met in Nuevo Cristóbal, Colon, Panama.

TRIGESIMA QUINTA SESION ANUAL DE LA CONFERENCIA ANUAL
PROVISIONAL DE CENTRO AMERICA

Designaciones para el Año Conferencial de 1968
Colón, R. de P.

COSTA RICA

Distrito de la Meseta Central:

Superintendente; Carlos Luis Jiménez M.

San José:

Iglesia «El Redentor»	Juan Sosa R.
Pastor Ayudante	Aurelio Retana
Hatillo y Alajuelita	Virginia Lane
Iglesia «San Pablo»	Carlos Luis Jiménez M.
Pastor Ayudante	A Suplirse
Guadalupe	Carlos E. Fajardo P.
«Unións Habla Inglesa	Marion F. Woods
San Pedro	Marion F. Woods
Pastor Ayudante	Claudio Soto O.

Alajuela:

Iglesia «El Mesías»	Jaime Staedeker
Pastor Suplente	Herbert Tavenner
Pastor Ayudante	Alexis Guevara
Esparta y Circuito	Carlos A. Vargas
Ciudad Quesada	José Murillo D.
Circuito San Carlos	Fernando Cerdas

Distrito del Pacífico:

Superintendente | Russell Sargent
Golfito y Circuito: | Russell Sargent

Pastor Ayudante	Russell Sargent
Palmar Sur y Circuito	Alberto Rivera
Puerto Cortés y Circuito	A Suplirse
Corredores y Circuito	Manuel Palacios
Pueblo Nuevo de Coto	A Suplirse
Esquinas	Martín Villachica
Laurel y Circuito	A Suplirse
Kilómetro 31 y Circuito	José B. Molina
Río Sierpe	Manuel Sanabria
Puerto Armuelles y Fincas	
Pueblo Civil (Golfito)	

Revdo. A. Rivera R.

Fotografía histórica tomada en la Conferencia de Colón, Panamá, en la que puede apreciarse al Obispo Jorge A. Miller, su hija Evelin y su esposo Jess Berger.

Iglesia y Casa Pastoral de Nuevo Cristóbal, Colón, R. de Panamá, en donde tuvo lugar la Conferencia de 1958.

Handouts from the Methodist Episcopal Conference of 1958 in Panama

Here are the handouts from that conference. See that

group on the top left? The guy in the front row, one person from the right, is Alberto Rivera.

See the listing of circuit preachers on the right page? Listed in Golfito and its circuit, under "Puerto Cortés y Circuito," is Alberto Rivera.

This started to really make sense. With the authority given him as a circuit preacher, Alberto could quickly affect a number of congregations, as many as were on his circuit.

He once said he messed up a good many churches. As a Methodist circuit preacher, he could enter quickly, cause havoc, and leave just as quickly to the next church in the circuit.

I'm not telling anybody what to believe. I'm just trying to make sense of what Alberto left behind.

And it all started with a photograph.

I think Jack did the right thing, staying polite, generous, focused on spreading the gospel, and printing Alberto's case against the Roman Catholic institution, the Whore of Babylon of Revelation 17-18. You can read the story for yourself in the Chick Publications Crusader Comics series on Alberto, and come to your own conclusions.

7

Observing the Little Things

When I first wrote the previous chapter, I made an American mistake. I read the date that Alberto wrote on the photograph for his father, 6/2/58 as June 2nd, 1958. But pretty much everybody else in the world knows that I got those numbers switched. Only in America do we list it by month first, then the day, then the year. Everywhere else it's listed by the day, then the month, then the year. So it's not June 2nd, 1958. It's actually the 6th of February, 1958.

It's still two months away from Holy Week, but now it's in the other direction. It's two months earlier, not two months later. I could never be a spy with an obvious American mistake like that. There is the story of one spy who was caught because he switched the knife and fork after he cut his meat, another distinctly American habit.

Jack was good at noting little things like that. One day he met a woman for maybe a minute and a half. Immediately afterward, Jack said "I noticed her face. Either she had chemo, or she was on psych medications." Bam! Nailed it! Maybe Jack was good at that, because he was both a skilled artist and an actor. And both helped him to identify tiny things about people quickly.

I'll tell you more about that. And I'll tell you about a

couple of nuns that picked out something interesting about Alberto Rivera.

In Jack's senior year at Alhambra High School he got into forensics, skilled public speaking. By March, 1942, he had become a finalist in the Forensic Tournament of the San Gabriel League. Jack's section was called the Humorous Declamation Division. That's where you recite something humorous written by someone else, maybe even well-known. And it is judged basically by how effectively your retelling of it moves the audience.

Now it was Jack's turn. He started in on his lines, then suddenly, everything went blank. Jack froze in position. His face, his body, all completely still. Then the words came back to him. So he resumed where he had left off and finished the speech. He was glad that at least he had gotten all his lines out. He didn't think that with a mess-up like that he had a chance.

When it came time to award the winners, a judge said to Jack in front of the crowd, "That was the most powerful use of a pregnant pause I have ever seen!" And Jack won 1st place in his division!

Forensic Tournament of the San Gabriel League

MARCH 23, 1942
(Date)

Award of Excellence in Forensic Competition

JACK CHICK —————— (NAME OF CONTESTANT)

has won _1 ST_ place in _FINALS_ of the _HUMOROUS DEC._ Division

League Officers:

_____
PRESIDENT

_____
VICE PRES.

_____
SECRETARY

J. Edmund Mayer
CHAIRMAN OF TOURNAMENT

Jack's 1st place award in his Forensics (speech) category, March 23, 1942

Jack (back right) and other award winners at Alhambra High in 1942

Here's Jack, with a number of other high school award winners. Jack's prize was a two-year paid scholarship to the Pasadena Playhouse.

The next year an aspiring actor was to make his debut performing at the Playhouse. Though he couldn't afford to be a student, director Gilmour Brown made him a director. His name was Raymond Burr. People now think of him as Perry Mason, or Ironside.

Jack took his first semester and started his second. But on February 1, 1943 he was given a formal invitation. Congratulations, Mr. Chick! You are qualified to serve in the United States Army. 18-year-old Jack was drafted —in the middle of World War II.

When Jack came back from the war, he got back into the program at the Playhouse. And he met two lifelong friends.

Jack with Rex Smith, friends for life, about 1948

The first was Rex Smith. They joked together, acted together, total friends for life.

**Rex (left) & Jack (right), in "Broken Dishes" at the
Pasadena Playhouse, 1947 or '48**

Jack (middle) and Rex (right), in "Broken Dishes"

Here they are in a Playhouse production, "Broken Dishes." Ironically, unsaved Jack is playing the minister.

Lola Lynn Priddle with Jack, late 1940s

The second "friend" was Lola Lynn Priddle.

Jack and Lola Lynn, March 22, 1948

On March 22, 1948 she changed her name… to Lola Lynn Chick! As an actor, Jack learned to observe behaviors, the little things that set us apart from each other, and that communicate a personality and even a story.

This is from a special memories book Jack made about the Playhouse days.

Jack's book about Playhouse life

Note Jack's first copyright, 1947

Jack always remembered the day he forgot his lines.

And we all know the second influence in his life: comic art. Jack started with airplanes and never stopped drawing.

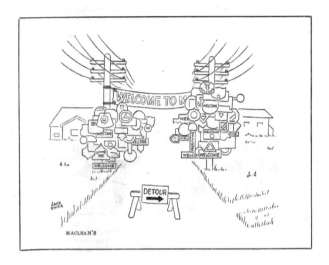

**Possibly Jack's first published work,
MacLeans, May 15, 1949**

In 1949, an early comic by Jack appeared in Canada's *Macleans* magazine. So his in-laws surely saw Jack's art there.

Jack noticed the subtle humor in things. So here you see a sign with every welcome possible – with a detour sign in front of it!

Welcome, but not welcome *right now*.

Even yesterday, Jack's friends retold the story, how Jack would be in a restaurant, or in the car and he'd say "Look at those ears!" "Look at that nose!" He was fascinated by differences between people, and then he would draw them.

Jack told me that early on he had drawn caricatures, and that is an art all by itself. He said it's very different from regular comic art. And he would have to work at it, if he were going to do it again. Jack observed people, and both his acting and public speaking, and even his comic drawing, helped him to be an observer of people.

When Jack would take people to lunch, Jack always noticed who was kind or unkind to the help. Jack didn't respect some major missionaries and preachers and authors, who would act all nice to Jack, but then be rough with the servers, or not even acknowledge their existence. Jack and I always made friends with the servers. Any of them reading this can tell you this is true!

He also observed Alberto. Yet Jack would be the first to admit that though he was raised around Catholics (still another story), he didn't know the nuances that, say, a nun would recognize.

Jack observed how people were treated

Page 4 March/April, 1988 BATTLE CRY

National Catholic Newspaper Admits Donna Eubanks Is Real

The nationally distributed Catholic weekly, OUR SUNDAY VISITOR, broke a long silence this month, to admit that former Catholic nun Donna Eubanks was really who she says she is. Donna is pictured in her habit in the five Alberto Series Crusader Comics along with her testimony that what Dr. Alberto Rivera is saying about the Roman Catholic system is true.

OSV admits, in a two-part article written by their west coast correspondent, Gerard Sherry, to conducting an investigation to verify Eubanks' testimony and found that it was true that she entered a convent in her late teens, became a teaching nun and later a sister superior.

Of course they repeat the story that they conducted a similar investigation into Alberto Rivera's background and did not find evidence that he was a Jesuit priest in Spain, as his credentials, reproduced in the Crusader Comics, prove. Rivera points out that they would not dare admit that he was a priest because it would then verify his story.

Much of the information in the articles was obtained by Mr. Sherry when he visited Chick Publications offices several years ago posing as a bookstore owner from Las Vegas. After obtaining access to Chick Publications offices, he continued to question office personnel and at no time did he reveal his real

She says, "Alberto is right"

identity. It was only after articles began to appear under his by-line in OSV, that his deception was discovered.

Besides the two-part series in OSV, other stories and comments are surfacing again about "Fundamentalist publisher Jack Chick" waging a "relentless war" of "bigotry" against the Catholic Church using "hateful little comic books."

Desperate attempts are made to link Chick Publications to recent scandals in spite of the fact that Chick Publications survives solely on the sale of tracts and books which are moderately priced.

Bible-believers can only expect a renewed attack from the ecumenical crowd. Recent scandals have handed them a golden opportunity to attack public enemy number one, the true Christian who dares stand up and call religious hypocrisy "sin."

There is a new wave of interest by the public media in "crimes of hate"

with several states strengthening their laws against violent acts motivated by "racial or religious hatred." Jesuit and other Catholic leaders all over the world, have labeled Chick tracts as "hate literature" and have successfully gotten them banned in some countries. The momentum is growing in this country to override our constitutional freedoms to preach the Bible without compromise.

This in spite of the fact that Chick Publications has gone out of its way in every tract and book to tell the truth in love, so that the precious people caught in this deception will not lose their souls to hell. The Bible says that all idolaters will be cast in the lake of fire (see Rev. 21:8).

Why do they scream "HATE LITERATURE"? If what Chick Publications has printed is scripturally wrong, why not just prove it wrong by the Bible and let it stand on its own merit? But they did the same to Jesus. They could not counter the piercing sword of the truth that He spoke. They could only attack His reputation and crucify His body.

But Jesus said that if they did it to the Master, how much more they will do it to His servants. They killed Him because of His stand against the hyprocritical Pharisees of his day. Should Bible-believers be surprised today to also be followed by a mob screaming, "Crucify?"

Battle Cry, March/April 1988 article vindicating Donna Eubanks

And that's where Donna Eubanks comes in. Even the Catholic reporter for Our Sunday Visitor, Gerard Sherry,

Jack & Donna Eubanks

Jack & Donna at her retirement

who lied and told Jack he was a Christian bookstore owner in Las Vegas, had to admit that Donna really was a nun of the Sisters of St. Joseph for 23 years, who was promoted to teaching nun and later to sister superior. She and her Catholic nun friend, Gracie, saw Alberto and instantly recognized he was trained as a priest.

Here at Chick Publications, Donna and Gracie would giggle and laugh, because they had this private little joke. They'd see Alberto walk and talk and behave in a way that was normal to him. And they'd call him, "His sacerdotal eminence" and laugh to themselves, when he'd leave the room.

As Donna said, it, "When he'd walk into the room, we would see: he was a priest! He acts like one. They have this manner about them that comes from years of being the head honcho. Their manner. It was bred into them."

Alberto had it. Donna said, "There's no doubt!" So Donna and Gracie had that private little joke. Because some mannerisms just don't go away that easily, we all have our behaviors that give us away. And according to two long-time, former nuns, Alberto had them.

Old habits don't die that easily. So it pays to observe, like Jack and Donna did.

8

Jack Leaves the Stage

From his Junior year at Alhambra High School, Jack was involved with acting. In 1941, he was already in the Wardrobe department. He's right there in the center back.

WARDROBE   ROW 1, left to right: Hassenplug, Fleming, Sec.; Harper, Treas.; Rockwell, V. Pres.; Muninger, Pres.; Brooks, Utell. ROW 2: Berryman, Harvey, Sinclair, Sneed, Chick, Hirsch, Barrow, Trailer, Nini.

Theatrical Trailers
Wardrobe, Make-up, Radio and Stage Crew

Jack in the Wardrobe department, Alhambra High School (1941)

Jack in the Light and Shadow drama club (1941)

And he was also in Light and Shadow. Again, right there in the middle.

Jack's senior picture, Alhambra High School (1942)

But it was in his senior year that he really began to shine. He was in the Masquers (Light and Shadow changed its name), still in the center.

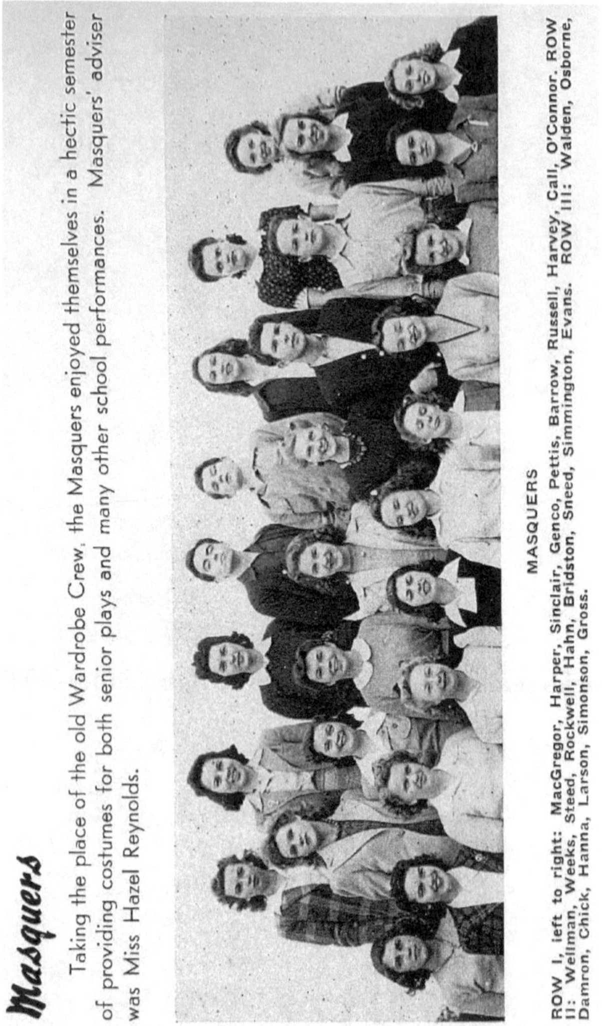

Masquers

Taking the place of the old Wardrobe Crew, the Masquers enjoyed themselves in a hectic semester of providing costumes for both senior plays and many other school performances. Masquers' adviser was Miss Hazel Reynolds.

MASQUERS

ROW I, left to right: MacGregor, Harper, Sinclair, Genco, Pettis, Barrow, Russell, Harvey, Call, O'Connor. ROW II: Wellman, Weeks, Steed, Rockwell, Hahn, Bridston, Sneed, Simmington, Evans. ROW III: Walden, Osborne, Damron, Chick, Hanna, Larson, Simonson, Gross.

Jack in Masquers drama club (1942)

But, Jack was also the commissioner of Forensics —public speaking.

Jack as Commissioner of Forensics (1942)

And in addition, he was in the Senior play, "The American Way."

Jack as Karl Gunther in "The American Way" (1942)

Jack was quite a dramatic actor.

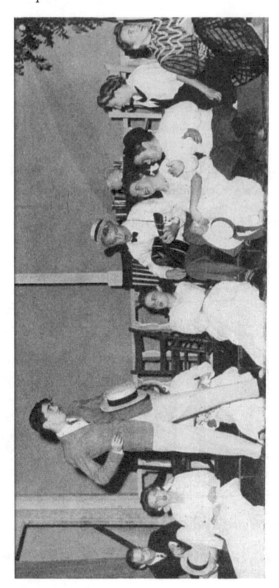

Another view of Jack in "The American Way" (1942)

The yearbook review said, "Jack Chick was outstanding in his portrayal of Karl Gunther."

It seemed that he was fast becoming a public speaker and actor. So it is no wonder that he won that scholarship to the Pasadena Playhouse, and continued, even after the war, to finish his two years' study.

Jack and Lola Lynn, and two men "out in the cold" (1946)

And he managed to get Lola Lynn away from all the other guys. That included his best friend, Rex Smith.

Rex Smith and Lola Lynn

It would take something major to get Jack to change from his —and Lola Lynn's— destiny in the motion picture industry. And something did.

Jack told me exactly what happened. And now I'm going to tell you.

After Jack returned from his honeymoon in 1948, he was a changed man. He was a saved man. He had become a Christian on his honeymoon. But that's another story.

Now, married to the love of his life, Jack told me he approached 20th Century Fox, to see about getting a start in Hollywood with his beautiful wife, Lola Lynn.

Jack left his new wife at home. When it was his turn, he was led into a producer's office. The producer was busy with another man, who obviously worked for him. The underling seems to have been a director. He was asking the producer about finding a job for a certain young lady.

The director said, "So, what do you think? Pretty good, huh?" The producer eyed her portfolio, and looked at the man directly. "Tell me. Has she made the rounds?" "Oh yeah, she's slept with about everyone in town." The producer eyed the director. "What about you? Has she been with you?"

"No…"

The producer closed the portfolio and handed it back. "Okay. When she's slept with you, then bring her to me. Then we'll see if we have something we can put her in."

Jack was sitting there with his hat in his hand, taking it all in. The director walked out and Jack stood up. "Jack," the producer began, "look. Times are hard at the moment. You look good, but let me be straight with you. We don't have room for you right now.

"Take Vincent Price. We had to let *him* go for a while. He went over to New York. So tell you what. Why don't you go to New York, make yourself a name, and then come back. We'll fix you up. Okay?"

Jack made a decision right there and then. "I don't want my wife to get mixed up in this." For the first time in his life, Jack realized how seedy and immoral Hollywood was. It really sank in, when he thought about what would happen to his wife on the way to her dream of being an actress.

Jack got up and walked out. And he never looked back. There was more to life than fame and fortune.

1 Timothy 6:10-11:

> For the love of money is the root of all evil: which
> while some coveted after, they have erred from the
> faith, and pierced themselves through with many
> sorrows. But thou, O man of God, flee these things;
> and follow after righteousness, godliness, faith,
> love, patience, meekness.

That led Jack to pursue the other talent he had cultivated since first grade, drawing. But that will take another chapter.

I will say this in closing. I tried to make a tract before I met Jack. I just couldn't do it. But when he let me start writing them, he said, "David, remember. You're the writer, the producer, and the director. You write the script. You choose the actors. You set the scenes. And you tell the story."

You see, God didn't waste a minute of all that Jack learned about acting. He re-purposed it to good use, making gospel tracts, and teaching me to do the same.

Next, I'm gonna tell you about how God saved his skin during World War II, and how God saved his soul after the war.

9

Twice Saved

Hand-to-hand combat practice

Jack Chick was a real man. He always worked hard. He tried to do the responsible thing, even before he became a Christian. But he was still an unsaved man. For me to tell this part of the story, you need to know a little more about what Jack was like, by his own admission, before he was saved.

So get ready to walk back into history —*his story*— told the way Jack told me.

Jack and I started working together in August of 2000. On the second or third day he told me he had never learned dirty words growing up. But his Catholic extended family did something awful. They wouldn't give young "Jackie" the food unless he took the Lord's name in vain.

He said they made him say, "Please pass the potatoes, blankety-blank!" They loved it. It made them laugh.

So Jack, who didn't get much attention from either his dad

or mom for various reasons, took the Lord's name in vain. That was one thing that his relatives liked.

But Jack's colorful speech was too much for the Christians at Alhambra High School. They wouldn't have anything to do with him. They didn't even tell him the gospel!

Think about that. So Jack didn't cuss like street kids. That

Jack tells his story

is, until he entered the military. He was sent "the letter" on February 1st, 1943. He said it was more like "Congratulations! You have been invited to serve your country."

He went into the recruiting office. And they were all, "Sit down, sir." "Thank you, sir." "Sign right here, sir." "Now go through that door right over there."

And once he walked through that door, everything changed. "Alright you blankety-blanks! You belong to the US Army now!"

And then he heard the most vile filth he had ever heard, and he heard it over and over, from the moment he walked through that door, to the moment after the last salute as he headed home.

Life at the barracks

Jack said, "We were called 'The Greatest Generation.' But we weren't great. We were filthy sinners, just like everyone else."

The soldiers in Jack's unit were also filthy in another area: fornication.

Jack told me horrifying stories about what servicemen did, first in New Guinea and later in Japan. Jack saw first-hand the horrible diseases they got from that debauchery.

Jack with some fellow soldiers (1943-44)

One of Jack's photos of the New Guineans

Some of the beautiful people Jack photographed in Japan

There are many beautiful people in Japan. And Jack told me the women were lovely. But they were not for him.

One night, the servicemen designated Jack as the driver (since he didn't drink) and they went out and got roaring drunk. Then they went into a brothel.

One woman came out to Jack. He told me, "She was the most beautiful young lady I had ever seen. She looked at me and pointed to her nose. She said, 'You want me?'"

Jack said, "No!!!" and pulled back, as scared as can be. He'd watched those Army films on the diseases people got from fornication. Jack hadn't met Lola Lynn yet, but he wanted to keep himself clean for his future wife.

This is the woman he was waiting for.

Jack's platoon. That's Jack on the far left. The suspected Mormon is in the hat.

I don't know how many professed Christians were among

the bunch of cursing, drinking fornicators in Jack's unit. But one thing I can tell you. There was one man who sat with unsaved Jack in the jeep that night. And he was a Mormon.

This might have been that guy.

This might be Jack's Mormon buddy

So Jack didn't drink, and he didn't go on the town. But he did take up swearing. And one more thing.

There weren't a lot of presents from home that came to servicemen. But one thing did come, and it came in boxes. Or more specifically, cartons. Every soldier was sent whole cartons of cigarettes. And the servicemen had nothing but time.

Jack signed up to go anywhere, for any duty that wasn't where he was stuck. But he was never assigned to any other unit. Of course, that saved his life. Almost everyone he knew who went into battle was eventually killed.

But in his whole enlistment, Jack never saw battle, not even once. Jack was never fired at. Jack never so much as saw a gun being fired at an enemy. Jack's assignment was cryptography.

So just like his army buddies, Jack sat and worked and

talked and smoked. And he picked up the habit of cursing with some of the new words.

Jack in full dress uniform

Jack rose to the rank of Sergeant before he was discharged on January 28, 1946, and continued studying at the Playhouse.

So in 1948, after the war, after graduating from the Play-house, and after getting married, he carried those two habits with him to Saskatchewan, Canada, when he met Lola Lynn Priddle's very conservative, Christian parents, Walter and Myrtle.

Walter and Myrtle Priddle, Jack's in-laws

Jack just looked and sounded like any other American sol-dier. But that didn't fly with these Canadian Christians. The very second day, Myrtle said to Lola Lynn, "What in the world did you marry?"

By Sunday Myrtle had had enough. She ushered Jack into another room, to hear the radio, Charles E. Fuller's *Old*

Fashioned Revival Hour. As he listened, Fuller quoted Isaiah
1:18:

> Come now, and let us reason together, saith the
> LORD: though your sins be as scarlet, they shall be
> as white as snow; though they be red like crimson,
> they shall be as wool.

Those words shot right through his soul and brought Jack
to his knees. It was crystal clear Jack was a sinner and he
needed forgiveness. He saw there was nothing he could do
to make himself good or save himself from hell fire and
damnation that his wife told him about.

You see, the Holy Ghost had used Lola Lynn a couple
of years earlier. Back when Lynn came to the Playhouse to
study voice and radio, Jack turned to her once and quoted
the popular saying from a song, "Don't be a fool, you fool."
Lynn turned to Jack, looked at him and said, "He who calls
his brother a fool is in danger of hell fire and damnation!"

So Jack fully felt the truth of Matthew 12:37: "For by thy
words thou shalt be justified, and by thy words thou shalt be
condemned."

Jack believed those words. And Jack believed Christ and
His sacrifice for his sins.

So that night on his honeymoon, Sunday night at 8:30
PM, right after the radio broadcast, Jack went into the
kitchen and cried out to God to save him.

And he did!

When Jack returned from his honeymoon later in 1948,
he was a changed man. That changed man went to 20th Century Fox, and quickly realized that he could never be part of
the filth of Hollywood.

God had saved his life in the war. Almost every single friend he made was killed on the battlefield. And now God had saved his soul from an infinitely worse fate: burning in the lake of fire.

One day, years later, Jack came upon one of those Christians from Alhambra High School. Jack asked him, "Why didn't you fellas ever tell me about Christ?"

The schoolmate told Jack, "We all said, 'He'd be the last guy on earth to ever accept Jesus.'" Well, "the last guy on earth to accept Jesus," received Jesus.

John 1:11-12:

> He (Christ) came unto his own, and his own
> received him not. But as many as received him, to
> them gave he power to become the sons of God,
> *even* to them that believe on his name:

Next, I'll tell you about how people reacted to Jack and his newfound faith, both back then, and right up to the present. And I'll show you how I, and all of Jack's friends, know he actually reacted to all the criticism he received.

10

Family Reactions

Hell is a real place. It is a place you want to avoid. Jesus shed His precious blood and died on the cross, to save us from hell. But many people use the word without thinking about its true meaning, like Jack's dad, Thomas Chick.

In mid 1948, when Jack and Lola came back from their honeymoon in Canada, Jack was a new creature, a saved man. And he was happy to share his newfound faith. But when they visited Jack's parents, as Lola Lynn walked in the door, Thomas, his dad, said to Lola, "Your mother sure as hell **ruined** my son."

This was the first of many reactions Jack —and his family— received simply because Jack followed Christ. How he held up through it all, is quite a story.

Infant Jack with mother, Pauline

Let me tell you a bit about Jack's mother, Pauline. Jack told me that one day his mother actually admitted that she tried many ways to abort him. He was unwanted. In fact, Jack said that whatever it was that his mom had done to him, it resulted in him having a number of ear problems when he was young.

Toddler Jack, and baby sister, Doris

Just like in the gospel tract, ***Unloved***, Jack was not the favorite child. His younger sister Doris was. But Jack just kept up his attitude and kept moving forward through life.

Many years later, when Pauline was in her late 70s, the

Alberto comic came out and the LA Times wrote a scathing four-page article about Jack and Alberto. Jack's mom called him and said, "Jack, don't tell anyone that I'm your mother."

When Jack gave her tracts and comics, she said, "I can't read them. They're wrong for my eyes and the ink isn't good for my fingers." But Jack knew she read lots of newspapers and magazines. It was

Jack's Mother, Pauline, many years later

just an excuse. Pauline Chick never supported her son. But none of that stopped Jack from continuing to stay focused on His Lord, and to get gospel tracts and comics and books written and in the hands of the unsaved and soul winners.

Jack had grown up around Catholics. In fact, his aunts and uncles were Roman Catholic. His aunt, who hated him, tried to push him to be nice to the local priest, who was a drunk who smoked, and a gambler. Jack was repulsed by his behavior.

And though even his sister might have been a Roman Catholic, Jack kept producing the Alberto series, through Part 6 in 1988. Pauline, Jack's mom, died in 1991. He truly wanted to win the precious Roman Catholics from their bondage to the Whore of Babylon.

Frame from Jack's first book, *Why No Revival?*

Let's go back to 1961.

Cover of first tract, *Why No Revival?*

When Jack wrote his first tract, ***Why No Revival***, he got great inspiration from the character faces of the people in the choir at his local church.

WHY NO REVIVAL ?

**Jack's characterization of the
church choir in *Why No Revival?***

But as soon as they recognized their faces, they gave Jack the cold shoulder. It's so ironic. In the years since then, people have been happy for, even begged for Jack to draw them in a tract, even as a villain. Times certainly changed!

The first review Jack got was by a Lutheran magazine. It lambasted Jack, telling how disgraceful and basically ungodly it was to put the gospel into a comic. Some Christian bookstores actually said it was "sacrilegious." But

**Original 1964 version
of the most famous
Chick Tract, *This Was
Your Life***

Jack just kept on making them.

Now let me tell you about his daughter, Carol.

In high school, she was ridiculed by her friends because of what Jack did for a living. A lady down the street befriended her. She was an old lady who used to be one of the Rockettes. She turned out to also be a Worthy Matron of the Eastern Star, who was still attractive enough to pick up young men in bars.

She turned Carol on to witchcraft. Jack would come home from work to find

Carol with her first husband

Carol with her second husband

various objects burned - or buried - in the backyard, and a growing collection of occultic objects in her room. Jack ended up throwing them out.

Carol's first husband got her pregnant —and then demanded that she abort the baby. Jack didn't find out about it until months later. That was the one and only time he could have been a Grandpa.

Carol's second husband was the son of a famous 1960s

Hollywood movie producer. Eventually he left her for someone else. Jack had tried to win this precious Jewish man to his own Messiah. But he was not interested. Carol was devastated. Years later, Jack said there were two men who craved her attention. One was a Christian man. The other was a "bad boy."

She chose the "bad boy." And it cost her, dearly. Jack traced the credit card statements that came to the house when she disappeared. He was taking all her money. He finally found her out of state. When he and a friend got there, the place was horrible.

She had been given chemical cocktails, and was already in a wheelchair. Her body had been destroyed. Jack took her frail body in his arms, back home, and cared for her, and got nurses for her. I can't even tell you what this bad boy was planning to do with her. By the way, Jack was powerless to prosecute that evil man, because he had immunity as an FBI informant. But that's another story.

This is what she looked like before.

Carol's last healthy picture, with Myrtle and Lola

And this is what she looked like after. Jack's old friend Rex spent time with her, a real Christian man.

Carol after her rescue

And while going to the store, getting supplies for the nurses, and picking up medicines, Jack still kept on writing tracts and spreading the gospel. This is one reason why Jack didn't spend much time in public. Carol died in 2001. She never reached 50. I was one of the people who played and sang at her funeral.

As you can see, Jack had no desire or time to respond to ridicule or give interviews. He did the Christian thing. He focused on his daughter and his wife.

So now let me tell you about his wife, Lola Lynn.

Lola Lynn

Jack, Lola Lynn and little Carol about 1956

As I told you, she was a beautiful lady, and she always looked like a movie star, even after Carol was born and grew up. But just four years after they got married, right after Carol was born, Lola got sick. Jack took care of Lola for 46 years. That's another reason why Jack wasn't seen much in public. He took care of his wife for decades, even before he rescued his daughter from that evil man.

Whenever Lola dressed up for church, it was a super-major endeavor, and only when she was physically able. It took so much, and yet she still looked her best, like this:

One of Jack and Lola Lynn's better moments

One Sunday when Lola spent hours getting ready, and Jack and she had come to church, the minister's wife greeted them. She said Hello to Jack, then turned to Lola, looked her up and down, and said, "Where have YOU been?" Those thoughtless words hurt both Jack and Lola.

Jack took her to more and more specialists. Finally he took her to a doctor in Mexico, driving her down and back, while not letting up on his work creating and drawing tracts, comics, and his major project, the film *The Light of the World*.

But one day his life was shattered. The Mexican doctor retired and his son took over. And he and a number of other people did horrifying things to Lola. When Jack picked her up, there was nothing he could do. The damage had been done. Lola had nightmares for years, waking up and flailing and hitting Jack without knowing it.

Lola Lynn enjoying Carol's birthday

And still Jack was patient and cared for her. Years later, she learned to forgive, and poured her love on her physically destroyed daughter. And Jack literally went to work, to the store, the pharmacy, and home, for years. In 1998 Lola Lynn was taken from him and found peace in heaven.

And Jack never turned from following Jesus, no matter what the enemy would throw at him and his family. Nor did he ever turn from his family. He was fiercely loyal to his God, to his family, and to his calling, Chick Publications.

Not everything has a sad ending. Let me tell you about Thomas Chick, Jack's dad.

Baby Jack with his dad, Thomas (1924)

Jack told me his dad didn't talk much to him. He was a sign painter, one of the top four sign painters in the Los Angeles area. He painted those signs people used to have in their stores, if you watch the old movies. Every day while sitting at the breakfast table, he'd practice making letters, like the letter O, over and over and over again. It looked like a million to little Jack.

He was always perfecting his work. I wonder if maybe Jack

wanted to copy his dad, and started drawing, so he would hold a pencil or pen, too.

Jack and Doris with their Dad, Thomas (early 1930s)

Here are Doris and Jack with their dad. See how he kept up his good attitude, despite being rejected by his own family? He carried that throughout life.

When he was first married, and didn't go to Hollywood, for a time he was a sign painter for his dad. Thomas gave him no privileges. He was treated as an employee only. "Time is money!" he'd say.

Jack told me he never even went to the bathroom the whole work day in the three or four years he worked for his dad. Not a single break. Not even to eat.

Jack carried that with him when he worked on a fully syndicated comic strip with his partner. But I'm saving that story for the next chapter.

Jack's parents, Thomas and Pauline, at their 50th wedding anniversary (March 19, 1973)

This picture was taken at his parents' 50th wedding anniversary, early 1973. It's the last picture he has of his dad.

In early November, Jack came to the hospital where his dad was dying. He could not talk. He didn't even move. Jack held his hand. Jack said to him, "Dad, I need to know that you will be with me in heaven. Please receive Jesus." Jack was holding his dad's hand.

"Look. I'm going to pray aloud, and if you want to receive Jesus, you can pray in your heart, with me, okay?"

"Dear Jesus, I am a sinner and I need forgiveness. I believe that You shed Your precious blood and died for me. Please forgive me, come into my heart and save me. Thank You. In Jesus' name, amen."

Then he turned to his dad, still holding his hand. "Dad, I hope you can hear me. Please, if you prayed with me and asked him to save you, please squeeze my hand."

And his dad squeezed his hand —TWICE! Shortly after that, Jack's dad died, forgiven.

With all that happened in Jack's life, he never stopped living for his Saviour who died for him. This is a typical picture of Jack in the office that I took from my desk.

Jack at his desk in the Chick Publications office (2007)

When Jack was on **his** deathbed, he still tried to draw a tract for him and me to work on… even after his hands were trembling. He never quit until his body did.

Jack's last tract cover idea (2016)

This is his last idea for a tract cover.

So if anyone says Jack was simply shy, or ungodly because he didn't go to regular church for decades, or cold hearted or mean, you can say to them: You don't know Jack.

Next, I'll tell you about the work Jack got done through all these years.

11

Unequally Yoked

When you have a man with drive and direction, a man really going someplace, people notice it. And some of those people might try to change his direction to somewhere he should not go.

So do you think that with Jack Chick's calling, the Devil wouldn't have taken notice, and tried to derail him? Wait till you find out some of the things the Devil tried to do against him.

Jack told me that, when he was a teenager, his Catholic aunt who hated him, pressured him to see a fortune teller. When he went in, the lady said she could see books —lots of books around Jack. She said he would be a famous author. And his books would go all over the world.

I remind you that teenager Jack wasn't a writer. He was an artist and a budding actor. Maybe devils can detect things about a person. They've been around about 6,000 years. Maybe there's something they can see in the spirit realm, I don't know. But the Devil somehow saw an inkling of Jack's destiny, and his minions acted upon that tip.

So Jack went on to start acting school in 1942, get drafted into the military in February 1943, finish acting school in 1948, get married to Lola Lynn late March, and by that fall leave the whole Hollywood career behind. Then for about the next three or four years he worked for his dad at his sign painting company.

But his direction in life never left him, not even in the midst of another job.

Front Cover **Jack's cartoon on the back cover of**
The American Cartoonist, **July 1949**

In the July, 1949 issue of *The American Cartoonist,* Jack got this comic printed on the back cover. Take a look.

A poor artist draws a tract with a wall full of rejection notices behind him. Then he goes to the mail box to put in his latest work. But in a stroke of irony, a mail truck speeds past him, hitting him. Then we see an editor who loves the work. And in the last frame, a postman walks away from a grave, and the artist, with joy holds the acceptance letter in his hand —as a ghost. He was finally recognized, after he had died.

Jack's ID card

Jack's 1949 comic illustrated an important truth. It's very hard to make a living drawing comics. Jack still needed a day job.

So in 1953 Jack got a job doing advertising art and other graphic work for Aerojet-General Corporation, an aerospace company in Azusa, about 20 miles northeast of Los Angeles.

Aerojet created rocket engines, and greatly assisted in World War II by the invention of the JATO engine, Jet-Assisted-Take-Off.

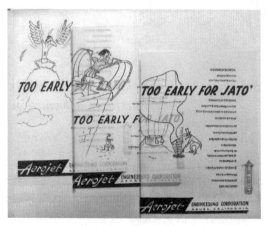

**Jack's advertising mock-ups to sell the
JATO engine to the government**

These are some of the advertising mock-ups Jack made for the JATO rocket, to sell the idea to various government buyers: Too early for JATO —showing historical attempts at flying, too early for a rocket engine for takeoff.

But Jack didn't think only of his day job and his family. He still wanted to draw comic art. He had already approached Coca Cola with an entire advertising idea, "Coke Around the World." He showed people in different countries drinking Coke within their own unique culture. After they watched his presentation, one of them said to Jack, "You're ten years too early. We're not ready for that yet."

Jack was ahead of his time a lot. That stayed a pattern in Jack's life. A few years later, Jack told me, Coke acted on his idea. But Jack didn't get any credit when they finally did it. In the meantime he kept trying out new ideas.

Late 1952-early 1953, Jack had floated a new idea to the Mirror Enterprises Syndicate of Los Angeles, now called *Times-Mirror*. His concept: to create a comic panel mirroring modern life, but in the costumes and setting of cavemen. Jack called it, "Times Have Changed?" Mirror Enterprises Syndicate bought the idea —but they wanted a daily comic, Monday-Friday, with a large, multi-panel color comic on Sundays, starting in the Summer of 1953.

For a big job like this, they wanted an ideas-man, who would feed new ideas and text to Jack, so Jack could focus on drawing them for 6 days a week.

**Jack with Bill Clayton at Jack's drawing board. Publicity
shot by the Mirror Enterprises Syndicate, 1953**

Enter Bill Clayton.

Whether Jack met Bill earlier, and he was Jack's contact
at the *Mirror*, or whether the *Mirror* recommended Bill to
Jack, I don't really know. But either way, The two of them
were joined together. But Jack was the only Christian. So
the advertising didn't go the way Jack would have written
it, at all.

Here is a quote from the *Mirror* promo article:

Have you ever said: 'Boy, times have really

changed.' Well, we have news for you. Times haven't changed as much as you may think they have, and if you don't believe us, just ask Bill Clayton and Jack Chick.

Through the use of an old, cracked crystal ball, an Ouija board left over from last Christmas, a dash of magic and a lot of imagination, these boys have been able to go back to the days of the cave man. And what did Clayton and Chick find when they turned back the clock over a million years?

CAVE MEN TO PROWL IN NEW MIRROR HIT

Have you ever said: "Boy, times have really changed."

Well, we have news for you. Times haven't changed as much as you may think they have, and if you don't believe us, just ask Bill Clayton and Jack Chick. Through the use of an old, cracked crystal ball, a Ouija board left over from last Christmas, a dash of magic and a lot of imagination, these boys have been able to go back to the days of the cave man.

And what did Clayton and Chick find when they turned back the clock over a million years?

Well, they found that things were a lot like they are today. This might sound hard to believe, but it's true.

To prove their point, Clayton and Chick have recorded all of the things they found when they returned to the cave man world. And, starting next Monday in the new panel feature called "TIMES HAVE CHANGED?" you'll be able to share the fun that happened when Mother Earth was a baby.

ARTISTS BILL CLAYTON AND JACK CHICK
You'll enjoy their funny panel, "Times Have Changed?"

Jack's copy of the ad for the "Times Have Changed?" comic panel, mid-1953

Well, they found that things were a lot like they are today. This might sound hard to believe, but it's true. To prove their point, Clayton and Chick have recorded all of the things they found when they returned to the cave man world. And, starting Next Monday in the new panel feature called, 'Times Have Changed?' you'll be able to share the fun that happened when Mother Earth was a baby.

To quote Fred Flintstone, "Hooo, boy."

Oh, and speaking of that, here is the main character

Glugford. That's Glugford, almost like Alfred, almost like … Fred.

And this is Irmug, almost like Irma, almost like… Wilma.

It was a completely new idea: a modern stone-age family. And Jack's art sold the idea. And this is the ad the *Mirror* sent to other newspapers:

The ad reads:

The main character, Glugford

3·4

"Times Have Changed?" is the first really different panel to come along in years. More than 40 leading papers bought it on sight on the basis of a few proofs and

Glugford's wife, Irmug

well ahead of first publication.

"Times Have Changed?" goes back to first principles of cartooning. It integrates the caption with the drawing. Every situation will strike home every day to every reader because it is one he will instantly recognize.

Times-Mirror **Ad to other newspapers for "Times Have Changed?" early 1953**

One of the things that makes "Times Have Changed?" so different is the wonderful backgrounds and the minor characters who people the panel. They give the reader a further series of chuckles after the initial impact of the caption."

The strip was a huge success. But Jack still had his day job. That December Jack drew a Christmas card for the guys at Aerojet.

Jack's Christmas card to employees of Aerojet, December 24, 1953

That's boss Bill Taft as Scrooge, Bill King, Kenny Seaman —and some dog. Yes, that was the first appearance of Fang, December 24, 1953, who has been hiding somewhere in most of Jack's Chick tracts ever since.

**Jack and Bill Clayton in another publicity shot for
"Times Have Changed?" early 1953**

In 1954, things changed. It turns out that Bill Clayton was
a Roman Catholic. He gave in to temptation. He didn't have

the indwelling Holy Spirit to stop him. So he went on the town and enjoyed his fame, instead of doing the hard work of coming up with ideas for Jack to draw in the panel. He left Jack to do everything himself.

A rare shot of non-smiling Jack under pressure at Aerojet

But Jack still had his day job. By day Jack was working at Aerojet, long, hard hours. Sometimes he was following blueprints for government projects, and sometimes coming up with advertising all on his own.

And by night, he wasn't relaxing and drawing new panels. No. He had to come up with all new ideas by himself, and compose how they would look, then draw them. That consumed both his nights and his weekends.

Lola, Carol and Jack, about 1954

Jack was unequally yoked, and in over his head. He was working to take care of his family. His wife was starting to be sick. He had a 2-year-old daughter. Something had to change. So in early 1954 Jack took readers' submitted ideas for panels, and then gave them credit.

May 5, 1954   June 24, 1954

July 14, 1954

Finally, Jack had it. He went to the *Mirror* and said, "I have to break my contract. I can't keep doing all the work myself."

But the executives at the *Mirror* said, "If you break your contract, Jack, you will never get a syndicated comic again." Something was about to break: either Jack or the contract. Jack broke the contract. That was the sad ending of being unequally yoked.

The ad copy was un-Christian, and his unsaved partner didn't have a relationship with the Father through faith in Christ to keep him from danger. When Bill Clayton didn't pull his weight, the partnership couldn't take the strain and finally fell apart.

Jack learned a valuable lesson. 2 Corinthians 6:14 "Be ye not unequally yoked together with unbelievers: for what fellowship hath righteousness with unrighteousness? and what communion hath light with darkness?"

If Jack were going to make comics, he'd have to do it himself, or with a reliable, Christian partner.

Next you're going to see how God used all of Jack's life-lessons, and some Chinese comic books, to bring Jack to the next stage in his life.

12

God's Plan Comes Together

After Jack broke his contract with Mirror Enterprises Syndicate, Jack's idea of a modern stone-age family didn't die. It was a major money-maker. ***But not for Jack.***

On February 17, 1958, Johnny Hart came out with the comic, "B.C." He kept drawing it until he passed away at his drawing board on April 7, 2007. It was one of the longest-running strips both

BC: Johnny Hart's stone-age comic characters

written and drawn by the original author. It was a great success.

Two years later, another "modern stone-age family," the Flintstones, debuted on September 30th, 1960 to April Fools' Day, 1966. It was the first prime time animated TV series, and the most successful animated fran-

Flintstones: TV's "modern stone-age family"

117

chise until The Simpsons in the late 1980s. TV Guide said it was the 2nd greatest cartoon series of all time.

Samples of Jack's "Times Have Changed?" Sunday comic

The ball that he started kept rolling for decades. That was Jack's gift to the secular world. Jack was ahead of his time. But when would it be Jack's time? You're about to find out.

Jack continued working for Aerojet-General through the 1950s.

December, 1954 Aerojet staff Christmas card

Here's his card for the Aerojet staff from December 1954. See Fang? There are a lot of mini stories going on here.

And here's the card from 1956.

1956 Aerojet company Christmas card

**Jack's boss, Bill Taft and wife, Ann,
on 1956 Christmas card.**

At Aerojet, sometimes the work didn't come. Jack told me, "That's the hardest time of all, when you have to look like you're working on a project, but you have to make it up." He explained that when clients come in, they can't see you sitting around with nothing to do. People who **have** contracts are more likely to **get** contracts.

So, the boss told Jack and the others to look busy. He literally had to make up projects and draw them. Sometimes this lasted for days or weeks on end, until the next project came. It was literally flood or famine.

But when they had projects, Jack shined. He was a hard worker. But realize, some of these were top secret projects. Sometimes they didn't even tell the graphic artists what they were putting together.

One day, Jack was curious. He stayed at work and started looking at all the smaller blueprints the others were working on. Then he made a master chart, putting all the component parts in their places. When he finished, he figured out they were working on a missile project.

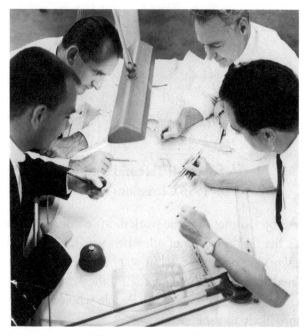

Jack working on blue prints with fellow graphic artists

The next morning he brought all the others around and showed them what he had found out. "So, *that's* what we've been working on!"

One day in 1958, Jack was given a special project. He was to make an animation that showed the benefits of Aerojet's infrared detection system. He was to show them how they could use the infrared system to detect ICBM missiles and other battlefield units.

Storyboard for weapon presentation

This is a storyboard he made for a scene called "Vulnerability." It was so good that in March 1959 the IFPA, the Industry Film Producers Association, gave him a Certificate of Merit for his training film, *Infrared*.

Jack's Certificate of Merit for the training film

But this wasn't what lit Jack's sparkler. He wanted souls to be saved. By 1960 Jack had gone from Aerojet-General in Azusa to Astro-Science in El Monte. Shortly after that, a Christian, George Otis, bought it.

One day during lunch an old welder gave Jack a copy of "Power from on High" by Charles Finney. As Jack used to say to me, "My sparkler was lit!"

Back at church he saw deadness and hypocrisy. Jack said, "That's why there's no revival!" The problem wasn't in the non-Christians. They were unsaved! What do you expect them to do but sin? But the Christians should set a good example.

So, Jack started sketching, illustrating Finney's words during his lunch breaks. He showed his sketches to Mary, a lady who ran a gospel bookstore in Alhambra. Here was a guy who was once syndicated in over 40 papers. But Jack was discouraged.

"Mary, I don't think anyone is going to publish these. They hit too hard."

"Why don't you publish them yourself?"

Jack kept sketching for a while, but then crumpled them up and tossed them in a trash barrel. But he still wanted to do God's will. And for once in his life, he asked God for a sign.

"Lord, if You want me to do this book, I need a verse about the leaven of the Pharisees and I don't know where it is."

There are 1189 chapters in the Bible, and more than that many pages. He shut his eyes and flipped pages, then stopped. He peeked with his left eye and there were the words, "beware of the leaven of the Pharisees."

Jack was on fire, and he started drawing like crazy. He got an $800 loan from a credit bureau and printed *Why No Revival.*

Cover of original large format booklet

As I told you in chapter 10, the Lutheran paper creamed Jack over it, saying it was "unrealistic." And the choir at his church recognized their faces and gave Jack the cold shoulder.

But Jack knew he did right. Still, he told me, "I wish I had known better and not put their faces in the tract."

What can you say? When Jack saw interesting faces, he drew them!

I wonder what they'd say now.

Right after this, he told me he was driving down the road and saw some teenagers on the sidewalk. He knew they were in rebellion, and he didn't like that at all. But suddenly the power of God hit him.

The reality struck him that they were lost and on the way to hell! He pulled over the car and just cried.

Then, like an entire story came into his head. Still crying, he got out his paper and pen and started writing as fast as he could. He could see it all. God poured it into his mind as he wrote. He called it, *A Demon's Nightmare.*

Why No Revival took weeks and weeks to write, both times. *A Demon's Nightmare* took just 15 minutes. Now he had his first gospel tract and no way to pay for it.

So, he went to his boss, George Otis. First, he gave a copy of *Why No Revival?* to George's secretary. Later, George

Original *A Demon's Nightmare*

called Jack into his office. He said to Jack, "My mother in law said you're a man of God and I should help you on your next printing."

Jack didn't even have to ask! God already had it all arranged.

As soon as he finished drawing *A Demon's Nightmare*, another idea occurred to him.

He had been reading Finney's Revival Lectures and wanted to get the message out. He would summarize its ideas and draw pictures to help explain them simply. So, he worked on this project every lunch and coffee break he got during the day, for months.

Someone saw that Jack's car was a Renault Dauphine. He said, "So, has yours caught on fire yet?" Evidently, they were well known for catching fire because of some defect.

Well, guess what? One day, just before Jack finished all his notes and drawings, someone said, "Jack —is that your car burning in the parking lot?"

Jack ran outside, past George Otis. "My car is on fire!" George said, "Well, who else's car would be burning?"

Jack said they squirted foam all over the car to put out the fire. Jack thought, "Oh no! All my work is gone!" But he had to check for himself. The car was coated in foam all over —except in the spot where the book and his Bible were. Praise God! Just one or two drops on his Bible, and *nothing* on his book.

Let's recap:

1961: *Why No Revival?* 10 inches wide.

1962: *A Demon's Nightmare*. 8 inches wide.

1963: what would Jack call this book that he was drawing? He had no idea. This is what Jack told me happened next:

"I walked out of the building, then it was like a whirlwind came down right in front of me. Sssssswish! And I heard a voice: 'THE LAST CALL.'

"Then I walked to my car. Sssssswish! 'THE LAST CALL.'

"Then I opened the door. Again, right in front of my car. Sssssswish! 'THE LAST CALL.'"

After that, Jack decided to call the new book, *The Last Call.*

The Last Call came out in 1963. Jack was running his fledgling company from his own kitchen table.

Soon, Jack had another idea for a tract. This one showed a person who went for what he wanted in this life, then died and was judged. Jack's wife, Lola Lynn, helped him with the Bible verses. She was a Bible verse factory. That helped Jack very much.

One of Jack's many church presentations.
From Crusader #19, *Unwanted*

He showed it the same way he presented company products to government buyers: by flipchart. Some of the people, including a pastor friend, remember Jack going to their churches and presenting the gospel by flipchart.

One man who viewed the gospel presentation was a member of the BGEA, the Billy Graham Evangelistic Association. He said, "Jack, the story you're telling is all about this guy's sinful life and judgment. Why don't you add a second section about what his life **could** have been like?"

The idea really struck Jack. He quickly wrote a second section: "This **can** be your life!"

In later 1963 Jack was invited to present the gospel to

Jack's original copy of
This Was Your Life

a group of inmates at a Prison Camp in the mountains above Azusa. Jack decided to try out the tract in flip chart form. Eleven prisoners attended chapel that night. When he finished, nine of them got saved!

So, Jack published the story as his fourth book, *This Was Your Life!* This is Jack's own 1964 copy.

Jack also used to meet people at Christian Businessmen's meetings where he visited and spoke.

China missionaries Bob and Helen Hammond

One day he spent some time with Bob Hammond, lifelong missionary and radio broadcaster of the "Voice of China and Asia." He told Jack that, in the 1940s, Communist spies saw how children in the United States were captivated by comic books.

They realized they could use comic books to win millions of Chinese children and adults to Communism.

And Bob Hammond gave Jack six of them as an example. Here they are.

Six titles used by the communists in China

Chinese pocket comics on the glory of Communism

But that's not all. What enabled them to spread so fast and overtake China was their pocket size. They could be carried with them and read wherever they were.

Jack eventually decided to start shrinking his tracts to just five inches wide, like the Chinese tracts. But not yet.

And this wasn't Jack's *only* iron in the fire. He was drawing for an aerospace company. But he still loved the idea of being an independent cartoonist.

Jack's local newspaper cartoon

So, he drew opinion pictures for a local newspaper around 1964. He got great reviews from readers.

Compliments Overdue for Chick

Dear Sir:

Compliments are overdue to "Chick" for his excellent political and sociological cartoons. His work is very profound and realistically to the point. Some of his characters are so delightfully humorous and so genuine that I find myself vacillating between laughing out loud or shaking my head in serious contemplation. Particularly meritorious was his cartoon in which a typical, law-abiding American family is pictured standing in the midst of placard-carrying misfits who are screaming for their rights. The woman sadly asserts to her husband, "The way things are going, I think we are the minority group."

It's very easy to experience empathy for this wife because our homes and businesses are surrounded by loud, ridiculous noises being emitted by minorities of so-called persecuted souls. The voices of these "nuts" are vociferous because their activities sell newspapers and air time. People, like the lady in the cartoon, are curious about the world we live in and this is a normal, healthy thing. The clamor of these "goofballs" doesn't really alarm me, but what is distressing is some of the recent Supreme Court decisions. Their apparent desire for a no-holds-barred atmosphere is giving impetus to the Communists, the racists, the paranoiacs, the criminals, and the sick personalities that plague every society.

It is time for the voices of the "square" majority to resound through the land. Counteraction to some of our contemporaries and their ill-informed flocks is desperately needed.

Once again, well done "Chick."

What ever did happen to the rights of the majority?

> Sincerely,
> Charles M. McDowell
> Glendora

On Cartoons, Politicians and Columns

Dear Sir:

First of all I would like to compliment the Tribune on its choice of cartoons on the Forum page. The new cartoons by "Chick" are refreshing and to the point. Almost every one of them is cut out and passed around to those who do not get the Tribune. I have a couple who are subscribing to the paper as a result of this. Again my compliments.

Secondly I would like to take issue with Thomas Lynch our attorney general. His proposal which is deadlocked in the State Senate which would make it illegal for two or more people to assemble with the intent of practicing military tactics can be a very dangerous law. Although it was proposed with good intentions, who would be the judge as to whether or not these people had intentions to practice military tactics? This is one of those proposals that look harmless enough but can be a powerful weapon to an unscrupulous politician to get rid of any opposition.

Thirdly I would like to comment on Drew Pearson's column. He holds that Red China has never been an aggressor and so he doesn't think they will start now. How shortsighted is he? Can't he remember the rape of Tibet? The slaughter of 30 million of their own? He says he holds no brief for Red China but his column makes him look as one of their major apologists. Wake up to the facts Drew and take a lesson in memory.

Thank you
Gary W. Anker
Rowland Heights

More Cheers for Chick's Cartoons

Dear Sir:

Thank you for printing Chick's cartoon of June 16, "Anyone like to give a short prayer before we outlaw prayer?" This is one time a picture has truly expressed a volume of truth.

The skeptics? Rosalie Gordon's "Nine Men Against America" will make believers of them as it did me.

Hope we will have more cartoons by Chick.

Sincerely,
Mrs. Josephine Baker
Glendora

Reader's comments on Jack's opinion cartoons for the
San Gabriel Valley Tribune

So, in 1965 he sent them to larger chains for syndication.

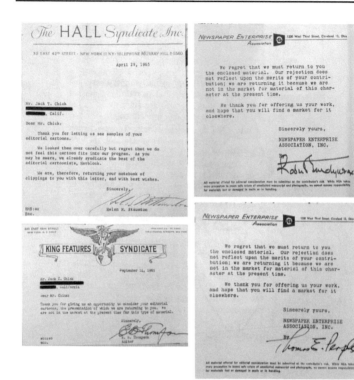

Rejection slips rejecting Jack's submissions

And he was turned down.

More Cheers for Chick's Cartoons

LI'L OL ORVIE
and the gunslinger

THE ID AND I

RAT RACE

"I SEE YOU'RE BACK AGAIN FOR
THAT LIVE LIVE LIVE FEELING!"

"My tranquilizer pills are simply wonderful!...my nerves are calm, my problems have vanished....and so have I!"

These are just some of the submissions —and rejections. The Mirror Enterprises Syndicate kept their promise. They made sure Jack wouldn't get accepted on any other syndicate.

A sample from Jack's portfolio for his "Even Then" comic proposal

He even made a variation on his original theme, "Even Then," which was based around Vikings, instead of cave men. But nobody wanted them. God had something better in view.

In 1966, Jack wrote *The Beast* —all 52 pages of it, and *Somebody Goofed.* Then Jack stopped. He left Astro-Science and went to Lockheed Aircraft.

And Jack made a decision. He couldn't do this alone. He had contracted with a bookstore distributor to supply his books to gospel bookstores. He rented a post office box to begin advertising.

But his company needed a name. Jack told me he was thinking of names like, "In Him," or "In Christ," or something.

While Jack was mulling the idea over, the printer said to him, "Here. I've already printed the tracts. You're Chick Publications." The printer named the company, not Jack! And it stuck.

Soon orders were coming in. He needed a partner —a *Christian* partner. He met co-workers who said they were Christians. Then he caught them doing things he didn't think glorified Christ, like gambling, and … other stuff.

Then, in 1968 he heard about another guy at Lockheed who was supposed to be a Christian. So, he found him.

"I hear you're a Christian."

"Yeah."

"Hi, I'm Jack Chick."

"I'm George Collins."

Jack handed George one of his tracts. George liked it. And that was the beginning of a lifelong friendship. They moved the business part from Jack's table to George's garage, and Jack went back to drawing more tracts.

Jack had shrunk the tracts to five inches wide. But one more thing happened.

Their printer, John Boewe, had set up a high-speed printing press to print a little bit smaller tract, one called *The Four Spiritual Laws* for Campus Crusade. He told Jack and George that if they could reformat the tracts to that size and just 24 pages, they could save a lot of money, sell them for a nickel, and people could easily put them in their pockets.

George Collins and Jack

Jack had a lot of reformatting to do, but it was a deal!

Then they sent out the newly reformatted tracts to a mailing list Jack had meticulously saved. And suddenly, as George put it, "Sales exploded!"

Lola Lynn, Jack and printer, John Boewe

Right away, they needed a staff. And they needed a place to put everything. So, they got a small office suite in Pomona. Then they needed another, then another.

A few years later, their printer died

and another took his place. He didn't share the same vision, and the prices were going to go way up. George had already thought ahead, and figured how they could get their own printing press to print them themselves.

Early logo used by Chick Publications

And that was when Chick Publications went into full swing as an independent publisher.

When people think of Chick Publications, I want them to realize that it's not a building. It's not a corporation. It's not even the people.

It's a vision to reach the lost, in the most efficient way possible, so that the most hurried, or shy person, can become an instant missionary, by means of low-cost, gospel tracts.

And Chick Publications is God's company. God put it together, and we pray for God to lead it throughout the next generation, just like He did, during Jack's lifetime.

Next you will find out about the preparations Jack made for the next generation, and how God chose me, of all people, to be Jack's friend and coworker.

13

Jack's Humility

It was August of 2000. I had just dismissed my bilingual (Spanish-English) kindergarten class. I matched up the last student with the last parent. Now it was time for a month-long break in our year-round elementary school in Fontana.

I closed the door and turned around. I heard a voice. "Go to Chick Publications at 3:00." There was no one in the room.

What would you do, if it happened to you?

Here's what I did. I got out my cell phone and called my wife Deborah. "Deborah, the Lord just told me to go to Chick Publications at 3:00."

"Well then, I think you'd better go to Chick Publications at 3:00." Deborah's very direct like that.

As I turned onto Archibald Avenue, where Chick Publications is, I said, "Lord, what's he gonna do? Offer me a job?"

I was preparing to be a 30-year teacher, like my mother. I wasn't prepared for what would happen next.

I had no way of knowing when Jack (whom I called, "Mr. Chick") was going to be in his office. In fact, I'd only seen him about four times before. I had no idea even when he was there, unless he came over and spoke to me.

I always went straight to my friend Ron's office, and I wouldn't even walk around. And that was only when I was invited in.

And though I'd written articles for the Battle Cry newsletter and published the ***King James Bible Companion*** five months earlier, I didn't feel I had any special privileges to just "walk around."

So I entered the small bookstore in front and stood there. There's a sign on the inner door that says "Please do not enter unless invited." I took that seriously. So I stood there, just for a moment, thinking to myself, "Okay, what do I do now?"

Just then, former nun Donna Eubanks, who worked at Chick, saw me. "David, come on back!"

That's unusual.

Donna Eubanks

Okay, but I still had no idea what was going to happen.

I followed her in to the art department, where the drawings and text are put together into the tracts. She sat down at her desk, and I stood by it for just a few seconds.

Then Jack came into the room. "David, come into my office. I want to talk to you." I am totally intrigued.

I followed "Mr. Chick" into his office. He had a white notebook open on his desk. It had his text and full-sized art for a tract called ***In the Beginning.***

"I want you to read this and tell me what you think."

So I read the tract. When I finished, I said, "Well, the only thing is this one date. When I studied evolution under Dr. David Jacobs at UC Irvine, he said it was "145 million years ago." Do you have a computer where I could go online and see if they've changed the date?"

Jack showed me to the customer service room, where they had one computer open. I looked it up, then came back. "No, they haven't changed it. That's still the date."

Jack said, "David, how would you like to work with me?"

How many of you would have said, "No"? Yeah, me neither. I couldn't wait to start!

I was just beginning a month of vacation, and I got to spend it with the very guy who wrote the tract, *This Was Your Life!* that God used to save me! But we didn't start writing right away. Jack had some things on his mind first.

(For this part, my wife Deborah and I only found out a few weeks ago the full story of why Jack asked me to work with him.)

As I told you, Jack prayed about everything. That's how things run here at Chick. Well, Jack had come to where he wanted someone to work with him. But it couldn't just be anybody. It had to be:

1) Someone who was there to help, not to tell Jack what to do;

2) Someone who wanted to learn, not pushing his own agenda; and

3) Someone easy to work with, not overly serious, except serious about souls.

Deb and I found out that Jack could hear when Ron (who's worked with Jack since 1970) and I would talk in his office. (I wasn't as quiet as I am now.)

Another of Jack's close friends actually suggested to Jack that he ask me to work with him, for a number of reasons. But Jack just responded, "I've got to pray about it."

And he did. Now he was going to see if I'd be a "fit." So, for the next three days, Jack just sat me down in front of him, and he proceeded to tell me his life's story.

Jack's friends are long-term friends. I found out from them that Jack was always forward-looking. He always looked to the next tract, the next comic book, the next project, always forward, never backward. He wanted to win souls. Looking backward didn't accomplish that.

So they didn't get to hear about much of Jack's past, or even know about it, except where they experienced it with Jack. But with me, Jack told me his life story. It was almost as if he knew what the future would bring. Or maybe God showed him something. I don't know.

As I told you in the beginning, Jack told me the good, the bad, and the ugly about his life. He told me about being betrayed by Christian leaders, the sinful behavior of famous ministers and people he'd known, and other behind-the-scenes stuff he knew about, lots of it because he was there. He also told me about many of the events I've been telling you in the last 12 chapters and the videos.

So after three days of piling on as much doom and gloom as he could (it seemed), he looked at me and said, "I bet you're pretty discouraged right now."

I answered, "No! I'm *en*couraged! Because if God spent all

those years of my life preparing me for this, then I believe God's going to do something with us!"

I spoke it from the bottom of my heart. And right after that, we started to write the Bible series of tracts. And Jack, who had been doing this for 40 years, actually listened to my tract ideas.

Set of 25 Bible series tracts

For instance, one day I told Jack that, 15 years before, my wife Deborah and I visited the MCC, the Metropolitan Community (LGBT) Church. Its founder wrote a book. I read it in the Fuller Library and wrote a report on my visit, for a class.

But I told Jack that MCC totally forgot a scripture —Jude 7. Jack listened. Then I went online to verify that they were still saying that stuff. They were. So that became the tract, **Sin City**.

Jack largely let me write **The Outcast, The Promise,** and others. He included my emotions about these topics into the tracts.

Jack wasn't proud. He was perfectly willing to listen to other people's suggestions. And he let me make or be a part of some major decisions from the beginning.

But in the end we wrote everything together. And Jack had the final say. We talked, acted out scenes, and there was lots and lots of laughing.

And lots of acting, too. I loved acting, from elementary through high school, and was once offered an agent as a kid.

But what I really love is telling stories. And that's what Jack and I did together: we acted out stories. Then we drew them on the white board, and then Jack or I took the sketches down on paper.

And he totally encouraged me to write books. He illustrated the first printings of ***Did the Catholic Church Give Us the Bible***, as well as ***Babylon Religion***.

He let me write comic books, as well. First, he asked me for my research and information on Mormonism for the comic *The Enchanter*. Then he basically let me tell the story, as well!

He just wasn't selfish, or in it for the glory. Here I'm a nobody and Jack lets me do all this. When I asked, "So who is the character going to be who gives the information to the Crusaders?" He said, "You. You're the one who knows this stuff."

So Jack did the main work on ***Unwanted***. I got to research and write ***Jesuits*** and ***Black Angel***, interviews and all. But we both researched and wrote ***Unthinkable*** together.

Jack didn't goof around. He was all about getting stuff done. He had an agenda every day. But it doesn't mean it was all serious. Jack had always been willing to pose himself or others in positions that helped him draw characters for the stories. Here are some examples:

This is from *The Secret of Prayer* (1972), found today in *The Next Step*, p. 27.

This is from *The Thing* (1971), p. 15

In designing the cover of ***Jesuits***, here is Jack's pose...:

...and the cover we didn't use!

God blessed me with being the one to introduce Jack to new technology. I always took my laptop to work, as well as my portable scanner.

Whenever a visitor had something interesting, I didn't photocopy it. I scanned it. I'm so glad. We might never have seen it again —and we usually didn't.

On June 15, 2006 at Chick Fil-A, I told Jack how cell phones could take your picture without you knowing it. Jack said, "You mean you could take my picture with that phone?"

"Yep, and I just did."

"You mean you could take my picture with that phone?"

One day I was reading a spoof about Jack in *The Onion*, called "Jack Chick Fil-A." And I asked Jack, "Did you notice? We ate breakfast at Flappy ***Jack's***, and now we're having lunch at ***Chick*** Fil-A!" We laughed. It hadn't occurred to us before.

We acted, laughed, joked —but all with a serious goal: the salvation of souls. We want to make tracts that make it easy for anyone to become an instant soul-winner, even when he or she doesn't have the time or the know-how. We try to pack as much as we can into a 24-page tract, but no more than 40 words per panel.

It takes a lot of prayer and a lot of hard work. We work on the tract the best we can, and check it the best we can, so you can focus on winning souls.

We even put as many scriptures as we can, to give the soul-winner or the lost person something he or she can look up and find answers that lead the lost to forgiveness in Christ.

Okay, I have to tell you, Jack originally wanted me to write a book, half about Jack and half about me. This is what Jack

originally wanted the book to be called: Little Jackie Chick and Me —And, Oh Yes... One Billion Gospel Tracts!

He'd even share his own biography! Jack didn't mind being little in his own eyes. Jesus Christ and His gospel —that is what God wants exalted.

And that's what kept Jack motivated.

One day when we were writing *Just One More*, a tract on drunkenness, Jack asked me to look up some statistics. When he saw the number of people who die per day on average, it really struck him.

He said, "All our tracts, all the souls we reach for Christ are just a drop in the bucket compared to all that are lost and going to hell."

Depiction of hell in *The Light of the World* DVD

That picture in his studio at his home kept him motivated to push forward, even when he was tired and his body was giving way to age. It is a zoomed-in part of one of the pictures for *The Light of the World* film.

So now you've gotten a glimpse into the Jack Chick I know.

I want to close this with an offer to you. After you've watched the vlog series and read this book, if there is a question that you didn't find answered, you can write to me at dwdaniels@chick.com.

If I see a particular question is being asked by a number of people, indicating widespread interest in that subject, I may select it to answer and post the answer in a video or web page so others can see the answer, too.

So, if you bump into someone or read someone's biography of Jack Chick, and it doesn't say the same thing as I've just shown you over 13 videos, and in this book, you can look them right in the eye, just like I can. And you can say, "You don't know Jack."

14

Jack as My Example

Jack repeatedly told me certain things about himself. First, he never claimed to be an intellectual or a theologian. He used to say, "My IQ was a flat 100." Second, he never claimed great strength. He used to say, "When I entered the Army I was 96 pounds soaking wet." Jack never claimed to himself brains or brawn.

Jack in the Army, trying to look brawny

Jack didn't come from a **broken** family. His dad and mom, Thomas and Pauline, stayed married till death. And Thomas was a hard worker. No one could dispute those things.

But Jack didn't come from a **loving** family, either —at least, not to him. His sister, Doris, seemed to receive the affection. Jack reflected some of that in the too-close-to-home tract **Unloved** (2004). He told me his mom hardly ever spoke to him.

And when she did, it was usually negative.

His dad only spoke to him about work and things that interested him. One time, however, he taught Jack how to box. One day Jack practiced, with his dad coaching him, up close in front of him. All of a sudden, by accident, a left hook caught his dad in the face. ***POW!*** Jack said all his dad's sinuses drained out at that moment! Thomas had had problems breathing for years. But no more. That one punch ended his sinus problems forever. And it ended the boxing lessons between dad and son, as well.

**Thomas and Pauline
Chick, early 1920s**

It seems that from birth, even Jack's own mother wanted nothing to do with him. But there was a bright spot. Jack's dad got saved on his deathbed, in an almost identical way to what we put on page 21 of the tract ***Born Wild*** (2012).

But God doesn't care if we're ordinary or not, intellectual or not, strong or not. God does extraordinary things with ordinary people. And the Lord doesn't let a minute of our past go to waste, either. God is able to use every bit of it for His glory in our Christian life and ministry, if we'll let Him.

That's what God did with Jack. God took an unsaved man

and saved him. He took a non-literary man and made him the most published living author. And he used his drawing, habit of hard-work, his military and acting experience to create a publishing company that would get the gospel into comic tracts that could be spread all over the earth.

That's how thousands and thousands of people, all over the earth —including me, just a few miles away— received Christ and were forgiven. Those tracts pointed us to simple faith in the shed blood of the Saviour who loved us and paid for our sins.

Jack wanted me to write this book to encourage you, not to brag about him. He told me to tell you that if God will use him, He will use you, as well. God will use for His glory any Christian who is willing to follow Him and seek Him with all of his or her heart.

Think about it. What if I had said "No," when God told me "Go to Chick Publications at 3:00?" What if I had said, "That couldn't be God"? Then I would have missed out on all that God had prepared for me. He might have chosen someone else! Thank God He made me ready for that day. Because God had already made that day ready for me.

What does God want to do with you?

God gave Jack the vision and the skill to draw and write stories. But it would have stopped right there, if Jack hadn't **done** something with what God gave him.

And Jack didn't do this alone. Even after God assembled a team to work with Jack and make the tracts, nobody would have gotten saved with them, if somebody didn't buy them and pass them out.

Thank God for that stranger who gave me *This Was Your*

Life on June 7, 1972. Forty five years ago, God started me on a track that put me where I am now.

God did His part. Jack did his part. We at Chick Publications are doing our part, continuing that vision.

What about you? Will you do your part?

Jack with his drawings for the tract,
***The Throwaway Kid*, December 5, 2012**

15

What About Fang?

No biography about Jack would be complete without telling about Fang. Why is he there? What was Jack's purpose in drawing him? And how come we find him almost everywhere?

A former CIA friend once told me, "You can tell a lot about a person by how he treats his animals." Well, let me tell you: Jack loved animals. And animals loved Jack.

Here's a picture of Jack as a teenager with his cat. Let me show you a few more of Jack's animals.

Here he is about 1943 with a dog that had befriended the soldiers where he was stationed during World War II.

He had many dogs over the years. Here's Lola Lynn with a few of them.

I first visited Jack at the small home he purchased with the help of the G.I. Bill. He lived in it from the early 1950s through his wife's sickness and passing on 46 years later, and through the years of caring for his daughter until she went to be with the Lord in 2001. And he still lived in that modest house until he went to see Jesus. As far as I know, they almost always had dogs.

When I went to Jack's house for the first time, I met Gem, short for Gemstone.

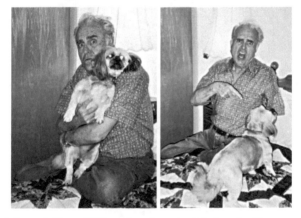

Jack loved Gem. When he played with her, he'd create silly roles for himself and include her in his antics.

That's the thing about dogs and cats. They always make cute faces and get your attention. That's exactly what Jack wanted to do with his drawings. As the Mirror advertisement for "Times Have Changed?" put it, the extra animals and people he drew "give the reader a further series of chuckles after the initial impact of the caption."

Jack wanted to draw the readers to the picture. And that's why he did that, all the way back in Christmas of 1953. Here is the full picture:

And here is a blown-up image of Fang.

The same in the 1954 Aerojet Christmas card. Here is the full picture.

And here is a close-up of Fang.

And he didn't confine his work to dogs. Did you notice what character he put in the "Times Have Changed?" panels?

"I'M TOO LIGHT A SLEEPER. I JUST WON'T LIVE SO CLOSE TO THE TRACKS!"

And here is the full panel out of Jack's collection, from March 4, 1954.

Jack's tiny characters interact with the story. They are not just "extra." When others, including Bill Clayton, tried to imitate Jack's style after he broke his contract, they just put in characters doing unrelated things.

But Jack made his characters part of the story. If his main characters were pretending to be "good," the kids were being awful. If something was drawn to complete the scene, the animals or other characters interacted with what was in the scenery. Get some Chick tracts and see for yourself!

Even in the 1960s, when Jack tried to make another comic strip called, "Even Then," for the newspapers, Fang made guest appearances. Here they are, for the first time.

Here is the cover of his proposal. Do you see Fang, twice?

Here is a close-up.

And these are a couple of Jack's original panels for "Even Then," here for the first time ever in print.

This one is from page 9 in the "Military" section.

From page 19, in the "Neighborhood" section.

ꝺOMESTIC

And page 22. This was the divider page for the domestic (home life) section.

While Jack and I worked together, we made friends with Kurt Kuersteiner of chickcomics.com. He has a whole "Chick museum" in Florida. On his website he lists Jack's tracts over the years, and he added a section, called "Fang's a lot! (An ongoing list of Fang sightings)"[4] Jack loved the idea! So with the help of the Art Department here at Chick, Jack had Fang inserted into lots of tracts that didn't have Fang to begin with!

---

4) It's found at http://www.monsterwax.com/fang.html

Right up to the last tract we made together, Jack found creative ways to sneak Fang into the picture. According to Kurt, who has checked every copy of Chick tracts, Fang first appeared in a tract in *The Mad Machine* (1975).

Kids love Fang. And for years people wanted to know the name of the cat, who also appears. A couple of years ago, in response to one customer who asked for a picture, Jack

named the cat, "Goldie."

So now you know it. The dog is Fang and the cat is Goldie.

I saw Jack after Gem died. He was sad. He loved his animals, and he wept when they died. He spent thou-sands of dollars on them when they were hurting. When they hurt, Jack hurt, too. I'm sure many of you know what that feels like.

After Gem died, Jack got Christy. Here Jack was, March 30, 2011, getting Christy to look at the camera for me. She's so cute! Everyone in our family fell in love with that fluffy little dog.

After that, Jack added two more dogs: Here are all three of them together, Christy, Angie and Cookie.

A few months ago Angie died. Jack wept. We all hurt for Angie's loss. She was the one who kept Cookie in line when she was young and feisty. I was glad Jack still had Christy and Cookie.

Jack had a few conversations with people before he died. The staff at Chick actually visited his bedside, and we spoke with Jack, and he spoke with each of us, the best he could.

I actually got to speak to him twice, two days in a row. He prayed for me a "double blessing," since he wanted me to continue after him, to write tracts and keep writing books and making videos. And I am happy to do so. I am so grateful for spending that time with him, and my family being able to visit Jack, as well.

One day, just before he went, this interchange took place between Jack and a loved one.

"You're gonna be alright."

"Where are you going?"

"I'm gonna see Jesus!"

Jack passed into eternity on Sunday night at 6:38, October 23, 2016.

According to his friends, when he breathed his last breath, Christy started barking and barking, running back and forth. I think she was saying, "Bring him back! Bring him back!"

Cookie laid down and cried, that whimpering cry that dogs do when they are sad.

Jack cried when his dogs died. And Cookie cried when Jack died.

Cookie mourned for three whole weeks. When my wife Deborah and I visited after that, Cookie had finished mourning and began to be herself again.

It's true. You can tell a lot about a person by how he treats his animals. And Jack was a very loving, caring, person. That's why he wrote gospel tracts. Because if Jack loved animals, how much more did he love people and care for their eternal destiny!

Every single person on earth is a person with a soul. And that soul has an eternal destination. Both are real. One is wherever the Son is, whether in heaven, on earth or the new heaven and new earth.

The other is hell immediately after death, followed in the end by judgment, then consigned to the lake of fire for all eternity. Judgment is a sobering thing for the Christian; but it's a terrifying thing for the unsaved. That's why God had Paul write:

"Knowing therefore the terror of the Lord, we persuade men...." (2 Corinthians 5:11)

If you who read this book have not dealt with your sins before God, then the only thing for you after death is punishment. But right now the door is open to you. Admit you are a sinner and that you know you need to be forgiven by God.

Confess the Lord Jesus, the Son of God, that He died for your sins and shed His holy blood to pay your entire sin debt. Ask Him to forgive your sins and receive the Lord Jesus as your Saviour. Then you to will have nothing to fear, not even death. And when you die, the Lord Himself will receive you into glory everlasting.

"...behold, now is the accepted time; behold, now is the day of salvation." (2 Corinthians 6:2)

God bless you, and have a wonderful day.

Tributes

After Jack's graduation to heaven, dozens of tributes flowed into the Chick Publications offices. Here is a sample:

Chick tracts has lost a warrior. We need to keep passing out tracts and winning souls for Jesus. Lord come quickly. *-R. Caillier*

I found some Chick tracts in my attic as a kid and knew my need of Jesus. Now I place Chick Publications - Chick Tracts every where I go. I take it as a mission, The Great Commission to go into all the world. *-C. W. Warner*

I've been a supporter of him and his work since circa 76. I remember hearing him talk about John Todd, Gavin Frost and Lynda Carter. *-J. Gale*

Jesus said that the world would hate us because we are of the light (Jesus). Jack was hated by some because he was a sold out child of God. And a lot of people say things because they are blind and in darkness. But he did what God wanted him to do. *-M. Lewis-Baptiste*

Very thankful for his contribution! Chick Tracts have had an impact on my life and I now hand them out; he left a legacy like no other. Thank you Jack Chick, enjoy the Lord! *-T. Cruz*

Mr. Chick was one of the most important influences in my life. I never met him in this life; but I have spent the past 15 years or so passing out his tracts. I loved Jack Chick. *-J. Mooney*

Brother Jack thank you so much for your tracts. We have given out thousands. To God be all the glory. Christ first all day -*T. Green*

Jack made a big impact on the world through his gospel tracts... Having shared his tracts and seen the effect they have has been amazing...What a blessing his tracts have been and no doubt continue to be so. His work inspired my own art when I was starting out evangelising through pictures. Now he is with the Lord in Glory! -*P. Millward*

So thankful to know he is in Heaven, with our Saviour. I am so thankful for his ministry here on earth. We absolutely love Chick Tracts, and will certainly miss him. Now we must pick up the mantel, and continue on serving the Lord. -*R. Bourque*

I remember, as a young man hitchhiking, a man gave me a Chick tract. I did not get saved for several years, but that tract got me thinking pretty hard about things. See you in heaven Jack and thank you. -*M. Dzieminski*

Jack Chick made a huge difference in my life. The Alberto series, the tracts, 50 years in the church of Rome, Smoke-screens, The Secret History Of The Jesuits. His publications molded and prepared me against a storm of lies. -*P. Dulz*

I was a fan of Jack Chick's work even before I became a Christian myself. And while I can't say I agreed with all (even most) of Jack's positions on social issues, he was a true and faithful servant of God who has gone on to a well-deserved rest and reward with our Father in Heaven. RIP, Brother Jack, and thank you for your uncompromising efforts in bearing witness to the gospel of Our Lord. -*P. Cortez*

I disagree with Jack Chick on a number of aspects of the Christian Faith, but one thing I don't think any of us can fault him on is the fact that he spent his life fully devoted to the God and gospel that he believed in. How many of us can say we are as devoted to our respective faiths as he was? I know I can't. -*R. Mayers*

Jack started a wonderful ministry! My church passes out Chick tracts to trick-or-treaters every year along with a cup of cider and candy. It is a good ministry outreach. God bless you David Daniels and the Chick publication ministry! -*D. Schoenhals*

RIP Mr. Jack Chick. I have handed out 100's of thousands of his cartoon tracts in New York. If one soul will be in heaven rather than going to hell it would be worth the effort to hand them out. Heaven and Hell are real places -*R. McDermott*

RIP Jack - your publications were well received around the world - and they gave people a choice - and that's all that is asked of anyone - to offer people choices - what they do with those choices becomes who they are -*F. Godon*

The LORD used Jack's tracts to lead me to repentance and salvation through faith in Him back in 1978. It totally changed my life. I'll be forever grateful to the Lord Jesus and for Jack's ministry. -*B. Harper*

I can well remember the very first time I ever saw a Chick tract. Someone had left it on a bench and I picked it up. The tract had no words, but moved me deeply, and caused me to think about eternal things like where I would go when

I died. A little less than a year later I accepted Jesus Christ as my Saviour and became a born again believer in Jesus Christ. The Chick gospel tract certainly played a role in that. Thank you, Jack Chick, for your years of faithful service to our Lord, before whose face you now stand. -*G. Grider*

I have Brother Chick as one more person to thank for bringing my husband to the Lord through his tracts. -*C. Rogers*

Condolences to the family of Jack T. Chick. Words cannot describe the positive impact he has had indirectly on my life. I was discipled through his many tracts and publications. Great will be his reward. - *S. Strong*

Chick Tracts reached my family, and relatives, as far as the gospel is concerned. It was during my senior year in high school, that I came to know Christ as my Lord and personal savior, through a coffee house ministry. Your tracts were a wonderful witness about Christ's love and salvation. 'THIS WAS YOUR LIFE', most definitely spoke to me about how I must plan for eternity, now, while God's grace allows it. Your 'LOVE STORY' tract, also, was a very special tract, that simply shared God's message of salvation, as well. May the Lord continue to bless your ministry, especially if the Lord tarries in His return. -*B. Bates*

From Trieste, Eastern Italy, near Slovenia: With emotion, I wish to thank Jack for all that he did, under the inspiration of the Holy Ghost, to bring relief and salvation in the utmost corners of this sad world. God bless you all. -*E. Roncelli*

First, let me personally express my regards over the passing of Jack Chick, because in the decades of reading his soul winning literature, I have grown a serious respect for this man, and I collect all his Chick tracts, which is my visual guide to God's laws and his awesome truths! I take this opportunity to express my grief over his passing—but I'm also happy, because I know that he is in the hands of his Lord, and he'll be rewarded for his many labors in saving people from Christless deaths through his outstanding tracts. I also hope that David Daniels will continue Mr. Chick's great work, in keeping the tracts published and distributed, despite a changing world, that has chosen to fall away from God's laws and ordinances. God bless you all, and especially with high condolences for Jack Chick's passing. May he find greater reward for all his wonderful soul winning works with Jesus Christ! -*J. Hill*

I would just like to send my condolences on the passing of Jack. I have been familiar with Chick publications since my childhood (I'm 43 now). My Dad always had Chick tracts and the very important Alberto series of comics in the house. I, like many others, drifted away from a Godly life for the better part of 30 years but, mercifully I came back to our Messiah a couple of years ago. Thankfully, due in part to Jack's work, my precious wife and kids were also saved and redeemed by the Blood of our Lord and Savior! Hallelujah! I will always use Jack's literature and look forward to his personal friendship in the NEW JERUSALEM! "Well done, my good and faithful servant" -*S. Machnau*

I was a teenager when I first read *This Was Your Life*. It scared the Hades out of me, I never thought about anything like that before, so of course it got me to thinking about death and where am I going to go, so anyways it really opened up my eyes and my spiritual side to be saved and live right, thank you Jack so much, and I'm sure I'm just one of many, many lives that Jack has changed. Blessing to you Jack and the Books still be published today -*C. Nelson*

Made in United States
Troutdale, OR
04/29/2024

19527642R00100